Navigating *through* Mathematical Connections *in* Grades 9–12

Maurice J. Burke
Ted Hodgson
Paul Kehle
Pat Mara
Diane Resek

Maurice J. Burke
Grades 9–12 Editor

Peggy A. House
Navigations Series Editor

NATIONAL COUNCIL OF
TEACHERS OF MATHEMATICS

D1211106

Copyright © 2006 by
The National Council of Teachers of Mathematics, Inc.
1906 Association Drive, Reston, VA 20191-1502
(703) 620-9840; (800) 235-7566; www.nctm.org

Library of Congress Cataloging-in-Publication Data

Navigating through mathematical connections in grades 9–12 / Maurice
   J. Burke ... [et al.].
      p. cm. — (Principles and standards for school mathematics navigations series)
   Includes bibliographical references.
   ISBN 0-87353-576-6
1. Mathematics—Study and teaching (Secondary)—Activity programs
—United States. 2. Problem solving—Study and teaching (Secondary)
—Activity programs—United States.   I. Burke, Maurice Joseph. II. Series.
   QA13.N387 2006
   510.71'2—dc22
                                    2005027662

The National Council of Teachers of Mathematics is a public voice of mathematics education, providing vision, leadership, and professional development to support teachers in ensuring mathematics learning of the highest quality for all students.

Printed in the United States of America

TABLE OF CONTENTS

CONTENTS OF THE CD-ROM

Introduction

Table of Standards and Expectations, Process Standards, Pre-K–Grade 12

Applets

Drug Dosage

Least Squares

Support Cables

Blackline Masters and Templates

All blackline titles listed above plus the following:

Centimeter Grid Paper

Readings from Publications of the National Council of Teachers of Mathematics

Drug Levels and Difference Equations

Kathleen A. Acker

Mathematics Teacher

Irrational Numbers on the Number Line: Perfectly Placed

Margaret Coffey

Mathematics Teacher

Match Making: Fitting Polynomials to Tables

Al Cuoco

Mathematics Teacher

About This Book

There can be no doubt that mathematics is a highly interconnected discipline. However, there is reason to ask whether mathematics teachers and courses customarily present the subject as a connected, integrated whole. *Principles and Standards for School Mathematics* (National Council of Teachers of Mathematics [NCTM] 2000) questions the effectiveness of "disintegrative" teaching and seeks to counter all such approaches with the Process Standards, which emphasize—

- Problem solving;
- Reasoning and proof;
- Communication;
- Connections; and
- Representation.

These processes for "doing mathematics" weave different content strands together into a coherent whole, and they stand behind the Curriculum Principle that *Principles and Standards* enunciates: "A curriculum is more than a collection of activities: it must be coherent, focused on important mathematics, and well articulated across the grades" (NCTM 2000, p. 14).

Teaching mathematical concepts in isolation, in restricted representational settings and formats that discourage connective processes, not only limits understanding but also diminishes interest in mathematics. George Pólya made the point succinctly: "Mathematics is interesting in so far as it occupies our reasoning and inventive powers" (Pólya 1973, p. 50).

This book shows how to embed connective processes in instruction to achieve coherence in the mathematics curriculum. To teach in the integrative ways that *Principles and Standards* emphasizes, teachers must exploit the frequent opportunities that real-world applications present for mathematical modeling and problem solving. Taking advantage of these opportunities is indispensable for helping students forge connections between mathematics and other disciplines, as well as within mathematics itself.

Overview of the Chapters

Navigating through Mathematical Connections in Grades 9–12 consists of four chapters, each of which presents a set of related activities for students. Ideas in the chapters build on one another, with each chapter supporting and enriching the next.

Chapter 1, "Connecting with Models," presents several examples of problems that invite mathematical modeling. The chapter highlights the integrative potential of such problems. By using mathematical models, students discover links between mathematics and other disciplines as well as interconnections within mathematics itself. The

"When students can see the connections across different mathematical content areas, they develop a view of mathematics as an integrated whole."
(NCTM 2000, p. 54)

problems in this chapter emphasize various stages in the modeling process.

Chapter 2, "Connecting with a Unifying Theme" illustrates the key role that a unifying idea can play in relating the structures in several mathematical content strands, including geometry, algebra, and statistics. The chapter highlights the potential of transformations to link the content strands in high school mathematics. Transformations serve to unify content not simply because they occur in many mathematical contexts but because they link mathematical structures in productive ways. The activities in chapter 2 emphasize the dual role of transformations: helping to forge the mathematical connections so vital to the restructuring in the modeling process, and demonstrating the coherence of the mathematics curriculum across grade levels.

Making a mathematical model for a real-world problem involves representing or replicating the situation of the problem in some mathematical way. Chapter 3, "Connecting with Multiple Representations," presents activities that highlight different aspects of the representational process. The first activity, Tiles in a Row, focuses on moving from a visual to an algebraic representation of a problem. The second activity, Measurement in the Round, focuses on moving from standard symbolic representations of mathematical functions to physical representations of them. The third activity, Transit Graphs, shows that linking simple mathematical representations of a phenomenon can lead to a new kind of mathematical representation that is very useful for solving problems.

When students apply connective cognitive processes to basic problems, rich, integrative problem-solving experiences can result. Chapter 4, "Connecting with Problem-Solving Processes," presents activities that illustrate some of the possibilities. By emphasizing aspects of the "looking back" phase of problem solving that George Pólya describes (Pólya 1973, pp. 14–19) these activities lead students to a deeper and more connected understanding of the underlying mathematics.

Using the book

The activity sheets that this book includes for students appear as reproducible blackline masters in the appendix, along with solutions to the problems. An icon (see the key on p. ix) in the margin serves to signal all the blackline pages, which teachers can also print from the CD-ROM that accompanies the book.

In addition to the blackline masters, the CD-ROM features special computer applets that complement ideas in the text and activities. Teachers can allow students to use the applets in conjunction with particular activities or apart from them, to extend and deepen students' understanding.

Readings for teachers' professional development also appear on the accompanying disk. A second icon in the text alerts readers to all materials on the CD-ROM.

Throughout the book, margin notes supply teaching tips and suggestions about related materials on the CD-ROM, as well as pertinent statements from *Principles and Standards for School Mathematics*. A third icon alerts the reader to these quotations, which highlight the fundamental notions that students should master the processes of mathematics and see mathematics as an integrated whole.

Whether a teacher uses a traditional mathematics curriculum or a curriculum designed to be "integrated," the processes that this book describes should become part of the fabric of the students' mathematical experiences. It is our hope that the examples in this book will guide teachers in integrating the content strands and processes of mathematics as *Principles and Standards for School Mathematics* recommends for all students.

Blackline Master

CD-ROM

Principles and Standards

Three different icons appear in the book, as shown in the key. One signals the blackline masters and indicates their locations in the appendix, another points readers to supplementary materials on the CD-ROM that accompanies the book, and a third alerts readers to material quoted from *Principles and Standards for School Mathematics.*

"Thinking mathematically involves looking for connections, and making connections builds mathematical understanding."
(NCTM 2000, p. 274)

NAVIGATIONS
SERIES

GRADES 9–12

NAVIGATING
through
MATHEMATICAL
CONNECTIONS

Introduction

Integrated Mathematics: Choices and Challenges (McGraw 2003) discusses many issues related to the development and implementation of integrated mathematics curricula. The introductory chapter, by Peggy House, appears on the CD-ROM that accompanies this volume.

All too often, mathematics educators think of integrated mathematics as just another curriculum option. However, in presenting and elaborating the Process Standards, *Principles and Standards for School Mathematics* (National Council for Teachers of Mathematics [NCTM] 2000) recommends that K–12 mathematics be taught and learned in an integrated, connected fashion, from prekindergarten through grade 12. This does not mean that *Principles and Standards* calls for teachers and schools to adopt textbooks titled "Integrated Mathematics," though such texts might have great potential for supporting the recommendations in the Standards. It does mean that teachers and schools should take advantage of the power of the Process Standards, which encompass connections, representation, problem solving, reasoning and proof, and communication. Teachers should use these Standards to link the mathematics curriculum's five essential content strands—number and operations, algebra, geometry, measurement, and data analysis and probability.

To become acquainted with the approach of this book and the topics that it covers, consider a well-known problem from the K–12 mathematics curriculum. Suppose that 500 mathematics teachers in an audience decide to shake hands. How much time will this activity take? The answer, of course, depends on how many handshakes the teachers give and what strategy they use to give them. Suppose that each of the 500 teachers shakes hands exactly once with every other teacher. How many handshakes will there be? An examination of several different strategies for solving this problem can illustrate the integrated nature of mathematics as well as highlight the themes of this book.

Combinatorial Strategy (S1)

A combinatorial strategy considers all the combinations of two teachers that we must make for each teacher to shake hands with every other teacher.

Enacting the problem

Once we have decided that every teacher shakes hands precisely once with every other teacher, we must determine an "enactment"—a way in which each teacher can shake hands with every other teacher, allowing us to make a count of the handshakes. To simplify the situation, we can start with a group of just five teachers and have every teacher shake hands once with every other teacher in the group while we count the handshakes.

In our simplified situation, the key is the same as in the original, more complex problem: we must make sure that every possible pair of teachers shakes hands. We could apply the same process to larger groups of teachers, but by *mathematizing* the process in the simplified case, we can discover how to use mathematics to find an answer to the original question.

Representing the problem mathematically

We can begin to treat the problem mathematically by applying a combinatorial strategy, which we will call S1, to our simplified situation. Our enactment of the problem suggests that a handshake corresponds to a single pairing of two teachers. We can think of each pair of teachers as a two-element subset of the set of teachers in the audience. The question then becomes, "How many two-element subsets are in a set with 500 elements?"

Restructuring the mathematical representation

The entries in Pascal's triangle tell us how many r-element subsets we can form from a set with n elements (see fig. 0.1). We call this number "n choose r" and denote it by

$$_nC_r \quad \text{or} \quad \binom{n}{r},$$

since we are counting how many ways we can choose a subset of r elements from a set of n elements. To solve our simplified case of five teachers shaking hands with one another, we find the entry that corresponds to a subset of two elements chosen from a set with five elements. This entry, 10, shows the number of ways of making such subsets from a five-element set. This number tells us that if in a group of five teachers, every teacher shakes hands with every other teacher, then the teachers will exchange ten handshakes in all.

To find

$$\binom{500}{2},$$

	Number (r) of elements in a subset						
$_nC_r$	0	1	2	3	4	5	....
0	1						
1	1	1					
2	1	2	1				
3	1	3	3	1			
4	1	4	6	4	1		
5	1	5	10	10	5	1	

Number (n) of elements in a set

Fig. **0.1.**

Pascal's triangle, presented as the entries in a table that gives the number of subsets with r elements, chosen from a set with n elements

or the number of handshakes that a group of 500 teachers would exchange if each teacher shook hands once with each other teacher, we would simply read from Pascal's triangle the number in the row labeled "500" and the column labeled "2." However, constructing Pascal's triangle for so many rows would be a prodigious task. Instead, we can use a combinatorial pattern that students in grades 9–12 frequently study:

$$\binom{n}{r} = \frac{n!}{r!(n-r)!}.$$

Thus, we can easily compute $\binom{500}{2}$:

$$\binom{500}{2} = \frac{500!}{2!\,498!} = \frac{500 \times 499}{2} = 124,750.$$

Resolving the problem

Since there are 124,750 two-element subsets in a set with 500 elements, we expect the 500 teachers to exchange 124,750 handshakes.

Ordered-Pair Strategy (S2)

An ordered-pair strategy considers all the possible ordered pairs of teachers and handshakes that we would need to form for each teacher to shake hands with every other teacher.

Enacting the problem

Working with the same five-teacher simplification of the problem as in S1, we could vary the enactment by using a slightly different process and implementing it to ensure that every possible pair of teachers shakes hands once. We would start our new process by numbering the teachers from one to five. We would have teacher 1 shake hands with every other teacher and then sit down. Next, teacher 2 would shake hands with every other teacher still standing, and then teacher 2 would also sit down. We would continue this process, counting all the handshakes at each stage, until we had all the teachers seated. We would get a total of 4 + 3 + 2 + 1, or 10, handshakes for the group of five teachers.

As before, we could use our enactment in the case of the 500 teachers, but once again doing so would be a formidable task. However, we can mathematize the process, and as a result, we can again discover a way to use mathematics to answer the original question.

Representing the problem mathematically

Our new enactment suggests the idea of representing a teacher and a handshake with an ordered pair of natural numbers. In the larger, original problem, we would represent each teacher by a natural number from 1 to 500, and we would then use these numbers to form an ordered pair (m, n) representing a handshake between teachers m and n. Since we begin with teacher 1, and no teacher shakes hands with himself or herself, m is less than n.

For example, in the simplified case of five teachers, the ordered pairs that result from the enactment are (1, 2), (1, 3), (1, 4), (1, 5), (2, 3), (2, 4), (2, 5), (3, 4), (3, 5), and (4, 5). Thus, we can restate our original problem as a new question: "How many ordered pairs of natural numbers (using the numbers between 1 and 500, inclusive) can we form in which the first number is less than the second number?"

Restructuring the mathematical representation

One way to answer this new question is to count the number of ordered pairs whose first coordinate is 1, add that to the number of ordered pairs whose first coordinate is 2, and so forth. In the simplified case of the five teachers, we get 4 + 3 + 2 + 1, or

$$\sum_{i=1}^{4} i.$$

In the case of 500 teachers, we get $\sum_{i=1}^{499} i.$

$$\sum_{i=1}^{499} i = \frac{500 \times 499}{2},$$

or 124,750 handshakes. Thus, the number of ordered pairs (m, n) of natural numbers where $1 \le m < n \le 500$ is 124,750.

Another way to count these ordered pairs of natural numbers is to invoke their correspondence with lattice points in the Cartesian plane. In the simplified case of five teachers, the ordered pairs representing the handshakes correspond to the lattice points shown in figure 0.2a. We can count these lattice points easily by considering the rectangular array in figure 0.2b. The geometry of the array reveals that the numbers of dark lattice points and light lattice points are the same. Thus,

Sums of integers and their powers have been studied extensively in the history of mathematics. Formulas for these sums appear in many high school algebra texts and are even programmed into graphing calculators:

$$1 + 2 + \ldots + k = \sum_{i=1}^{k} i = \frac{(k+1)k}{2},$$

$$1^2 + 2^2 + \ldots + k^2 = \sum_{i=1}^{k} i^2$$

$$= \frac{(2k+1)(k+1)k}{6},$$

and so forth.

there are $(1/2)(5 \times 4)$ dark lattice points. With 500 teachers, the resulting array would have 500 rows and 499 columns, yielding $(1/2)(500 \times 499)$, or 124,750 dark lattice points.

By studying the pattern of dark and light lattice points, we can see that the geometric strategy is equivalent to adding the numbers from 1 to 499 twice and then dividing by 2, a method attributed to Karl Friedrich Gauss for summing the integers from 1 to n (see fig. 0.3). We note that the columns of lattice points in figure 0.2b represent adding the terms from 1 to 4 in descending order (the dark lattice points: $4 + 3 + 2 + 1$) to the terms from 1 to 4 in ascending order (the light lattice points: $1 + 2 + 3 + 4$). The result is 4 columns, each with 5 lattice points, or a total of $(n - 1)(n)$, or $(4)(5)$, lattice points.

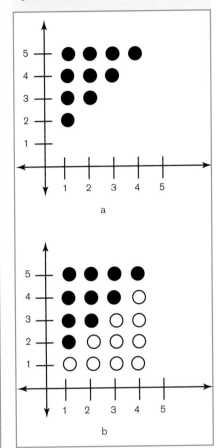

Fig. **0.2.**

Arrays of lattice points, showing (a) ordered pairs (m, n) representing teachers and handshakes in a group of five teachers, and (b) the rectangular array of which these ordered pairs are part

Fig. **0.3.**

The sum of the integers from 1 to $n - 1$. Adding the terms in the first two expressions for the sum yields the expression in the third line for

$$2\sum_{i=1}^{n-1} i,$$

which simplifies to the expressions in lines 4 and 5.

$$\sum_{i=1}^{n-1} i = 1 + 2 + \ldots + (n-2) + (n-1)$$

$$\sum_{i=1}^{n-1} i = (n-1) + (n-2) + \ldots + 2 + 1$$

$$2\sum_{i=1}^{n-1} i = n + n + \ldots + n + n$$

$$2\sum_{i=1}^{n-1} i = (n-1)n$$

$$\therefore \sum_{i=1}^{n-1} i = \frac{(n-1)n}{2}$$

Resolving the problem

However we count the ordered pairs, we get the same result:

$$\frac{500 \times 499}{2},$$

or 124,750, ordered pairs. Therefore, we would expect 124,750 handshakes.

Graph-Theory Strategy (S3)

A graph-theory strategy considers all the segments that can connect two vertices representing any two teachers in a simple graph of the handshake situation.

Enacting the problem

We can represent yet another way of enacting the handshakes and counting them by drawing a picture of the situation. Figure 0.4 presents a drawing that shows each teacher in our simplified group of five as a dot and each handshake as a segment connecting two dots. By counting

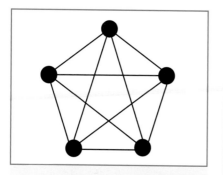

Fig. **0.4.**

A drawing to represent five teachers and the ten handshakes that occur when each teacher shakes hands with each other teacher

the segments, we arrive at the number of handshakes. We could use the same drawing process to handle the case of 500 teachers, but, once again, doing so would be impractical, and we choose instead to mathematize the process. By analyzing our mathematical model for the simple case, we again find a way to use mathematics to solve the original, larger problem.

Representing the problem mathematically

The drawing in figure 0.4 lets us think of the 500 teachers as vertices in a graph and a handshake as an edge containing exactly two of the vertices. With this representation, the question about how many handshakes the teachers exchange is transformed into a new question: "How many edges are in the graph?"

Restructuring the mathematical representation

From graph theory, we know that when every edge in a graph connects exactly two distinct vertices, the number of edges in the graph is one-half of the sum of the degrees of the vertices in the graph. The *degree* of a vertex is the number of edges containing the vertex. The graph in figure 0.4, which represents the simplified handshake problem, is called a *complete graph*, since exactly one edge connects each pair of vertices. (Every pair of teachers shakes hands exactly once.) In a complete graph with n vertices, each vertex must lie on $(n-1)$ edges and therefore have degree $(n-1)$. Thus, the sum of the degrees of the n vertices is $n(n-1)$, and the number of edges is

$$\frac{n(n-1)}{2}.$$

Resolving the problem

Since there are

$$\frac{500 \times 499}{2},$$

or 124,750, edges in a complete graph with 500 vertices, then there should be 124,750 handshakes among the 500 teachers.

Function Strategy (S4)

A function strategy considers a rule that relates the number of teachers to the number of handshakes that all the pairs of teachers exchange.

Enacting the problem

To enact the handshake problem in still another way, we could start with one teacher in the room. With one teacher, we would have 0 handshakes. Then we could have a second teacher enter the room. With two teachers in the room, we would have 1 handshake when the teachers shook hands precisely once. We could then have a third teacher enter the room and shake hands once with each of the two teachers there, for 2 new handshakes. Thus, when there are three teachers in the room, there are 3 handshakes. We could record these handshakes in a table like table 0.1. We could then have a fourth teacher enter the room and shake hands with each of the three teachers there, while we added these 3 new handshakes to our total and recorded the result.

We could, of course, continue this process until we had all 500 teachers from the original problem in the room. However, we prefer to mathematize the process and apply our mathematics to the larger problem.

Table 0.1.
Handshakes between Pairs of Teachers in a Room

Number of Teachers in Room	Number of Handshakes
1	0
2	1
3	3
4	6
5	10
⋮	⋮
500	?

Representing the problem mathematically

This enactment of the problem leads us to treat the number of handshakes as a function of n, the number of teachers in the room. Table 0.1 presents a function table for the problem. With this enactment, the question changes again, now becoming, "What function $f(n)$ fits the data in the table, and what is $f(500)$?"

Restructuring the mathematical representation

From the results that we recorded for our latest enactment, we see that $f(1) = 0, f(2) = f(1) + 1, f(3) = f(2) + 2 = 3, f(4) = f(3) + 3 = 6$, and so on. The emerging recursive pattern, $f(n + 1) = f(n) + n$, or $f(n + 1) - f(n) = n$, makes sense, since the $(n + 1)$th person shakes n hands on entering the room. We add these n handshakes to the total of the handshakes, $f(n)$, which we counted when there were only n people in the room.

We can identify $f(n + 1) - f(n) = n$ as a difference equation. The theory of difference equations tells us that when the difference between consecutive terms in a sequence, or $f(n + 1) - f(n)$, is a linear function of n, the sequence $f(n)$ is a quadratic function of n. Thus, since $f(n + 1) - f(n) = n$, we know that $f(n)$ is a quadratic function; in other words, $f(n) = an^2 + bn + c$, for some real numbers a, b, and c.

We can use many methods to find a, b, and c. For example, we can use a quadratic regression on the ordered pairs in our function table. Or we can use the function table to set up and solve a system of three equations in three unknowns. A third possibility is to use methods from the theory of difference equations (see Cuoco's [2003] discussion of Newton's difference formula). All these methods lead to the same result:

"In making choices about what kinds of situations students will model, teachers should include examples in which models can be expressed in iterative, or recursive, form."
(NCTM 2000, p. 303)

Cuoco (2003; available on the CD-ROM) discusses using Newton's difference formula as a simple way to fit a polynomial to a table.

$$f(n) = \frac{1}{2}n^2 - \frac{1}{2}n.$$

Resolving the problem

Since

$$f(500) = \frac{1}{2}500^2 - \frac{1}{2}(500),$$

or 124,750, there are 124,750 handshakes when 500 teachers are in the room.

Integrating Mathematics

Our consideration of multiple approaches to a simple problem illustrates some important things about mathematics. The handshake problem involves teachers and a handshake relation. Solution strategies S1–S4 model this phenomenon in four different areas of mathematics. Indirectly, these areas are linked through their connection to the handshake problem.

These connections should not surprise us. Much of mathematics has blossomed from the efforts of men and women to model the real world. In fact, one can argue that the drive to model the physical world—a goal of a vast array of sciences—has been a primary force in the genesis of many mathematical ideas, their structures, and their interconnections. It is the rule rather than the exception that real-world problems can be modeled in several mathematical domains, and the resulting mathematical models, in turn, reveal interconnections among these areas.

Our multiple models for the handshake problem illustrate some fundamental principles of mathematical modeling and of problem solving. Mathematical modeling of a real-world phenomenon consists of a process of representation, in which a model in a mathematical domain replicates the key elements and relations in the phenomenon. The choice of a mathematical representation often depends on how someone conceptualizes the problem and its components in an enactment. This enactment is an integral part of the process of representing the phenomenon and allows for multiple modes: kinesthetic, visual, verbal, and symbolic.

Though the handshake problem makes the choice of a representation look relatively simple and straightforward, the process typically demands an involved analysis of the real-world situation. A cycle of assumptions and refinements customarily characterizes this analysis, and it is this process of rethinking, revising, and refining that gives mathematical modeling its justly deserved reputation for fostering interdisciplinary thinking.

The representational stage in the mathematical modeling process leads to a restructuring of the problem in the mathematical realm. This mathematicizing facilitates the deduction of new relationships among the key elements in the model. The restructuring often takes multiple paths, as in the ordered-pair strategy (S2) and the function strategy (S4).

"Students in grades 9–12 should develop an increased capacity to link mathematical ideas and a deeper understanding of how more than one approach to the same problem can lead to equivalent results, even though the approaches might look quite different."

(NCTM 2000, p. 354)

Finally, the resolution phase translates the results of the model back to the original problem and validates them there. Here again, the handshake illustration makes this stage look easier than it ordinarily is. The process is usually involved; validating results depends on the adequacy of the assumptions underlying the representational stage and often leads to further refinements in the model.

The handshake problem also reveals that the modeling process can be useful in probing mathematical as well as real-world phenomena. The process can highlight connections in the mathematical world as well as between the mathematical world and the real world. For example, in S2, lattice points in a graph modeled the ordered pairs of teachers and handshakes. We then used the geometry of the graph to answer the question about the ordered pairs.

The practice of reserving the expression *mathematical modeling* for applications of mathematics to real-world phenomena is not uncommon, but this book is less restrictive in its use of the expression *modeling process*. The thought processes involved in modeling—whether one applies them to a real-world situation, like the handshake problem, or to a question about some mathematical phenomenon—are as intrinsic to mathematical thinking as assimilation and accommodation are to human learning.

The modeling process has exerted a powerful integrative and generative force on mathematics throughout history. For example, Descartes's modeling of Euclidean geometry's elements and relations within the domain of ordered pairs of numbers and their algebraic relations led to a historic restructuring of geometric questions in an algebraic framework. This restructuring ultimately resulted in the resolution of significant geometric problems. Descartes's groundbreaking work also led to a number line that included the negative numbers—a development that produced a momentous restructuring of algebra. Negative numbers had appeared in algebra before Descartes but were not widely accepted until after Descartes's innovation.

The history of imaginary numbers was similar. After emerging in algebra during the sixteenth century, these numbers did not gain wide acceptance among mathematicians until Wessel and Argand (ca. 1800) introduced the complex plane as a geometric model of the numbers and their operations.

The work of Beltrami, Klein, Riemann, Poincaré, and others can serve as a final example of the power of mathematical models to connect mathematical domains. These mathematicians created Euclidean models for non-Euclidean geometries. When the models established the independence of Euclid's parallel postulate from his other postulates, they greatly elevated the status of non-Euclidean geometry.

An integrative, problem-solving habit of mind

In addition to illustrating the integrative power of the modeling process, the handshake problem highlights another vital, integrative force within mathematics: the habit of mind that the mathematician brings to the problem-solving process. Pólya (1973) described this habit of mind most impressively, observing that to the mathematician, "no problem whatever is completely exhausted" (p. 15). Connective

"Students can use insights gained in one context to prove or disprove conjectures generated in another, and by linking mathematical ideas, they can develop robust understandings of problems."
(NCTM 2000, p. 354)

cognitive processes characterize the mathematical habit of mind. It uses deduction and proof to establish and organize interconnections among mathematical domains. It looks back at solutions, ever vigilant to find alternative, more effective ways to solve a problem and to see a solution at a glance. It extends and generalizes results to other problems within the same mathematical domain or, by analogy, to problems in other domains. It values conciseness, simplicity, and clarity in solutions—not only in notation but also in results.

It is this habit of mind that this book aims to cultivate, urging teachers to focus attention on the processes of representing and restructuring a problem—even in situations that do not involve real-world applications—while continuing to stress core, unifying concepts. Finally, the book emphasizes the importance of problem solving itself, which encourages reasoning and proof, exploring alternative routes, extending and generalizing results, and communicating results in simple, concise, and elegant ways.

NAVIGATIONS SERIES

GRADES 9–12

NAVIGATING *through* MATHEMATICAL CONNECTIONS

Chapter 1
Connecting with Models

Principles and Standards for School Mathematics (NCTM 2000) recommends giving students at all levels opportunities to learn about mathematics by working on problems that arise in contexts outside of mathematics, including their daily lives. Few educators would argue with the assertion that an emphasis on real-world applications is sound pedagogy.

Mathematical modeling provides a powerful means of integrating mathematics with other disciplines. This chapter presents activities that engage students in making mathematical models of real-world processes, such as inflating balloons, administering prescription drugs, and establishing territorial boundaries. By allowing your students to work with such contexts, you can help them discover that mathematics offers an effective and efficient tool for representing, analyzing, and predicting patterns in real phenomena from diverse realms of experience.

A modeling activity typically addresses a question that emerges from a particular contextual focus. To understand the context, you and your students will often need to consult reference materials or outside experts. This aspect of modeling makes it an ideal activity for integrating mathematics with other subjects. You will discover that the need for reliable, specialized information about a context frequently promotes opportunities for meaningful team teaching.

Because your purpose as a mathematics teacher is to provide opportunities for learning mathematics, you will want your students not only to develop a mathematical representation of a real-world situation but also to consider the model itself as an object of mathematical study. To be sure that your students are giving attention to both the correspondence

Few educators would argue with the assertion that an emphasis on real-world applications is sound pedagogy.

of the model to the real situation and the mathematics of the model itself, urge them to consider such questions as the following:

- How does the model operate?
- What aspects of the model represent reality?
- Can we restructure the model to shed light on the questions at hand? If so, how?

To use modeling successfully in instruction, be certain that your students maintain this dual focus on the real-world setting and the mathematics that describes the setting.

This chapter presents three activities that are similar to ones in a variety of curricular materials for grades 9–12, resources on the Internet, and books for high school mathematics teachers. In the first activity, Growing Balloons, students use regression techniques to model experimental data and call on proportional reasoning to assess the validity of their models. In the process, they discover the difference between empirical and theoretical modeling. In the second activity, Healthy Dose, students determine an effective and efficient dosage for a prescription drug, integrating empirical and analytical techniques in a context that is highly accessible. The third activity, Nearest Neighbors, focuses on geometric models that result from a simple rule for a "fair" distribution of territory. Each of these activities allows students to raise important questions about the real phenomena under investigation and interconnect a variety of mathematical tools in novel contexts.

Growing Balloons

Goals

- Construct an empirical model of a balloon's "growth"
- Construct a theoretical model of a balloon's "growth"

Materials and Equipment

For each student—
- A copy of the activity sheet "Breath by Breath"
- A copy of the activity sheet "Take a Breath and Theorize"
- A graphing calculator or access to spreadsheet software

For each group of three students—
- An uninflated balloon (which, when inflated, will be as nearly spherical as possible)
- A tape measure with centimeters and millimeters calibrated

pp. 88–89; 90–92

Discussion

Mathematics teachers and science teachers often approach modeling tasks with different objectives. On the one hand, modeling in the mathematics classroom may involve collecting data, displaying them graphically, and searching for a formula or function to describe them. Validating the results often entails gathering additional data and comparing the function's predictions with the actual outcomes. Models of this type, which typically use regression, residual analysis, and other data-driven techniques, are known as *empirical models* (Edwards and Hamson 1990).

On the other hand, scientists seek to discover relationships among experimental variables. For instance, the inverse square law depicts the relationship between the intensity of light (I) and the distance (D) from the light to an observer, with k as a constant of proportionality:

$$I = \frac{k}{D^2}.$$

Other formulas may fit data about light intensity and distance adequately and may even predict other results with sufficient accuracy. The inverse square law, however, not only fits the data well but also depicts a relationship *in theory* between D and I that is consistent with other accepted theories about light. Models of this type, which are often deduced from scientific principles and describe a relationship between two variables, are known as *theoretical models*.

Growing Balloons allows students to integrate empirical and theoretical modeling processes in one two-part activity. In both parts 1 and 2, the students model the relationship between the number of breaths that someone blows into a spherical balloon and the resulting circumference of a great circle of the balloon. Part 2 of the activity challenges the students to make connections between the theoretical and empirical models that they have made.

The parts of the activity show stages in the process of model development—a process that in fact is often cyclical. Someone devises a

The experiment in Growing Balloons is similar to one in "What's Your Orbit" (Systemic Initiative for Montana Mathematics and Science [SIMMS] 2003).

theory that suits the empirical data on hand, then collects new data and uses them to test the theory, and then, depending on the results, modifies the original theory. This cycle of collecting data, testing, and refining continues until a satisfactory theory emerges. In part 1, "Breath by Breath," students seek an empirical model of the relationship between the experimental variables—the number of breaths and the balloon's circumference. Variations in their methods of data collection are likely to result in several competing models. In part 2, "Take a Breath and Theorize," the students assess these models in the light of "theory" about the relationship between the circumference of a perfectly spherical balloon and the number of breaths of constant volume that someone might use to inflate it.

Part 1—"Breath by Breath"

Students collect data in part 1 and use them to develop insights into the theoretical relationship between the growing circumference (c) of a balloon and the number (b) of equal-sized breaths that somebody blows into it one breath at a time. Working in groups of three, the students begin the activity by selecting one group member to inflate the group's balloon, breath by breath, and a second group member to measure its circumference after each breath. The third member of the group records the group's data.

To develop an understanding of the relationship between c and b, the students must try to make each breath contribute the same volume of air to the balloon. For reasons of hygiene as well as for uniformity in the data, have just one group member inflate the balloon. Breath volume may differ significantly from person to person and so from group to group. Table 1.1 depicts sample data from one group of three students.

Table 1.1
Sample Data from Students for the Balloon Experiment

Number of Breaths	Circumference (cm)
1	21
2	28.5
3	32.5
4	37
5	39
6	41.5
7	43

Encourage your students to use a variety of techniques (for example, visual analysis or residuals) to identify a function that describes the trends in their data. Prompt them to assess the behavior of each function that they identify by considering such questions as, "Does the function continue to make sense beyond the range of the data set?"

Figures 1.1 and 1.2 show two competing functions on TI-83 Plus calculator screens. Figure 1.1 shows the quadratic function $y = -0.50x^2 + 7.56x + 14.50$, and figure 1.2 shows the power function $y = 21.54x^{0.37}$. Both functions appear to fit the data. However, if the balloon continued to grow indefinitely (though we know that it cannot), the power model would more accurately reflect the long-term behavior of the circumference of the balloon as a function of the number of breaths. Students conclude part 1 by explaining how well their function models their data.

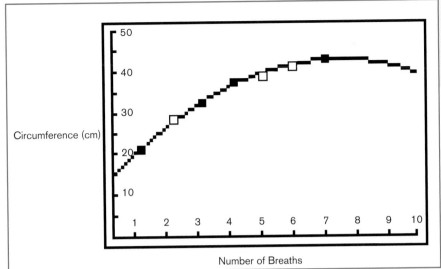

Circumference (cm)

Number of Breaths

Fig. **1.1.**

A scatterplot of the sample data with a graph of a quadratic regression function ($y = -0.50x^2 + 7.56x + 14.50$) that fits the data

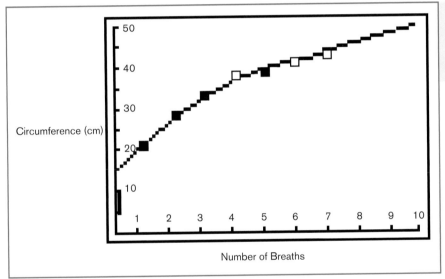

Circumference (cm)

Number of Breaths

Fig. **1.2.**

A scatterplot of the sample data with a graph of a power regression function ($y = 21.54x^{0.37}$)

Part 2—"Take a Breath and Theorize"

Part 2 of Growing Balloons turns the students' attention to theoretical relationships. To prepare your students for this work, direct them to reflect on their observations from part 1. Ask, "In general, what is the shape of the graph of your function relating the circumference of the balloon to the number of breaths?"

In the balloon experiment, the students probably obtained data that they could model in a graph like that in figure 1.3, which shows the circumference growing at a decreasing rate as the number of breaths increases. Many equations can yield such graphs, which you can use to introduce a discussion of the theoretical principles that underlie the phenomenon.

It is important for students in grades 9–12 to recognize that developing a theoretical model often involves proportional reasoning. A brief review of proportionality may be appropriate before your students begin the activity.

Fig. **1.3.**

The underlying shape of the relationship between the circumference of the sample balloon and the number of breaths blown into it

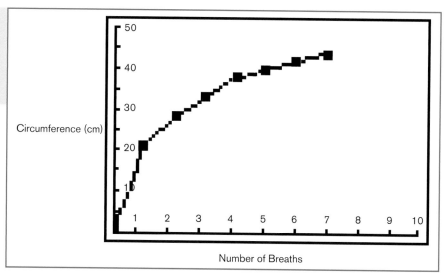

A linear function of the form $y = mx$, where m is a nonzero constant, is called a *direct variation*. If such a relationship exists between x and y, y is said to be *directly proportional* to x, and m is called the *constant of proportionality*, or the *constant of variation*.

Before students test for a proportional relationship, they must make a conjecture about the manner in which two variables are proportional to each other. They might assume that y is proportional to x, or to the reciprocal of x, or to the square of x, for example. A theoretical model often emerges from such conjectures. Proportional reasoning, which *Principles and Standards* recommends that all students learn to use proficiently, provides a powerful tool for connecting mathematics and real-world phenomena.

The students should know that variable quantities x and y are directly proportional to each other if, and only if, $y = mx$, where m is a constant. If students are testing for direct proportionality between variables that represent real data, they should also know that—

- the units of the y variable must be the same as those for mx;
- a scatterplot will show that the data lie approximately on a line through the origin.

In part 2, the students investigate whether a proportional relationship exists between c, the balloon's circumference, and b, the number of equal-sized breaths that someone uses to inflate the balloon. Before testing for a proportional relationship, the students must make a conjecture about the manner in which the two variables might be proportional to each other. The activity leads students to conjecture that c is proportional to $\sqrt[3]{b}$.

To help the students make this conjecture, the activity opens with a simple unit analysis. The students reflect on the fact that they tried to make all the breaths of air in part 1 the same volume. They can treat this volume theoretically as equivalent to a constant number (k) of cubic centimeters. Thus, at each stage ($b = 1$, $b = 2$, $b = 3$, etc.) in their balloon's growth, they can think of the balloon's volume, in theory, as equal to $b \times k$. This product is also equivalent to a number of cubic centimeters, since b is the number of breaths and k is equivalent to a particular number of cubic centimeters per breath. Thus, the students can see that $\sqrt[3]{bk}$ is equivalent to a length in centimeters. By reflecting that they measured the circumference (c) of their balloon in centimeters, they can speculate that c is related in some way to $\sqrt[3]{b}$, since $\sqrt[3]{bk} = \sqrt[3]{b} \times \sqrt[3]{k}$, and $\sqrt[3]{k}$ is a constant.

Numbers 1 to 6 on the activity sheet help the students use algebra to explore the assumption that c is proportional to $\sqrt[3]{b}$. Depending on the mathematical maturity of your students, you may need to modify these steps or closely supervise their work on them.

The key assumptions in the investigation involve the size of each breath and the shape of the balloon. By assuming that each breath adds the same unit of volume to the balloon, we can think of the balloon's volume as directly proportional to the number of breaths: $v = kb$.

Furthermore, by assuming that the balloon is spherical, we can calculate its volume (v) as equal to $\frac{4}{3}\pi r^3$,

where r is the radius of the balloon. This allows us to relate the circumference to the number of breaths:

$$v = \frac{4}{3}\pi r^3 \Leftrightarrow r = \sqrt[3]{\frac{3v}{4\pi}} = \sqrt[3]{\frac{3kb}{4\pi}};$$

hence,

$$r = \left(\sqrt[3]{\frac{3k}{4\pi}}\right)\left(\sqrt[3]{b}\right).$$

Thus, since $c = 2\pi r$, we conclude that

$$c = 2\pi\left(\sqrt[3]{\frac{3k}{4\pi}}\right)\left(\sqrt[3]{b}\right) = m\sqrt[3]{b},$$

where

$$m = 2\pi\left(\sqrt[3]{\frac{3k}{4\pi}}\right).$$

The assumptions that the balloon is spherical and that each breath adds the same volume of air lead to the theoretical model $c = m\sqrt[3]{b}$, which indicates that a balloon's circumference is directly proportional to the cube root of the number of breaths that someone uses to inflate it. Figure 1.4 depicts a graph of this relationship for one value of m. Although such a graph is not a proof of a relationship, it typically corresponds to the pattern in students' data for the balloon experiment.

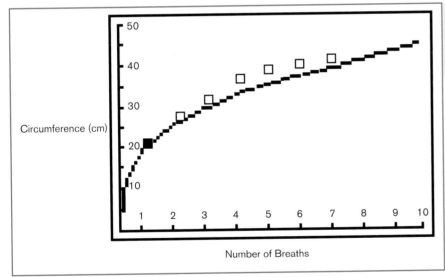

Fig. **1.4.**

A scatterplot of the sample data with a graph of $c = m\sqrt[3]{b}$ for $m = 21$

Students should use their data to determine the constant of proportionality m. One method for doing this is to create a scatterplot comparing c to $\sqrt[3]{b}$ and then estimate the slope of the line passing through the origin that best fits the scatterplot (see fig. 1.5). This method is an important one for students to know.

Some confusion may arise as your students compare the scatterplot depicting c versus b and the scatterplot depicting c versus $\sqrt[3]{b}$. However, understanding the relationship between the two scatterplots is crucial

Fig. **1.5.**
A scatterplot of $\left(\sqrt[3]{b},\ c\right)$ with a line of fit
through the origin

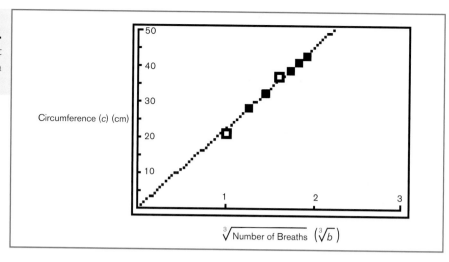

to a student's ability to use graphical methods to explore proportional relationships between variables.

The last question in the activity asks students to compare their theoretical and empirical models. Making such a comparison will lead them back to the original assumptions underlying their models. In discussing and investigating these assumptions, questions about physics, measurement, and mathematics will naturally arise. This step in the activity deserves more time than one might think, judging by the small space that it occupies on the activity sheet. The theoretical model supports the empirical work for the sample data in the solutions. In the theoretical model, the circumference of a great circle of the balloon is proportional to the cube root of the number of breaths. In the empirical model, the exponent of b, the number of breaths, is 0.37.

As a result of measurement errors and variation in the volume of air contained in each breath, you and your students can expect some differences. In addition, the shape and elasticity of the balloon will affect the model. Nonetheless, students are often surprised by the close correspondence of their empirical and theoretical models.

Assessment

This activity calls for several important skills and understandings that you can assess as your students work. Consider the following questions in evaluating their performance:

- Are the students able to produce appropriate graphs and construct functions that fit the data?
- What methods do the students employ for comparing functions with respect to their goodness of fit?
- How well do the students understand proportionality in graphs, equations, and real data?
- How well do the students understand unit analysis and use it to make inferences about possible relationships in the data?

One assessment strategy that you might use is to have each student produce a lab report of his or her group's experiment, detailing data, analyses, and conclusions. Your colleagues in the science department might have some good advice about how to use this method of assessment and what to expect from such an assignment.

Where to Go Next in Instruction

The activity Growing Balloons has provided a context for integrating mathematics and science through empirical and theoretical modeling of a simple phenomenon. It also illustrates a general point for students. It shows them that science is rich with theoretical models, many of which they can examine through empirical techniques.

In the next activity, Healthy Dose, students investigate patterns of change in a quantity—in this case, the amount of a prescription drug that remains in a patient's body at the end of a specific interval of time. This activity offers another scientific context in which proportional reasoning plays an important role.

Healthy Dose

Goals

- Use empirical and theoretical approaches to develop solutions to a drug dosage problem
- Use technology to investigate possible solutions to a drug dosage problem
- Develop and apply recursive representations to study change in a quantity

Materials and Equipment

For each student—

- A copy of the activity sheet "Experimenting with a Dosage"
- A copy of the activity sheet "Fine-Tuning a Dosage and a Schedule"
- Access to the applet Drug Dosage (available on the CD-ROM; optional)

For each group of three students—

- Access to spreadsheet software or a graphing calculator with data-analysis capabilities

Discussion

In this activity, the students model a commonplace situation in the world of medicine—the accumulation of a prescription drug in a patient's body and the elimination of the drug over time. Electronic spreadsheets (or other data-analysis tools) can make the activity accessible to a wide range of students. The problem that the students examine in Healthy Dose is richer than it at first appears and can lead to an understanding of a variety of complex mathematical concepts. For instance, the problem can allow students to identify patterns in data, construct recursive models, and analyze long-term behavior in the models.

Unlike the activity Growing Balloons, Healthy Dose does not ask the students to gather real-world data. However, just as in part 2 of Growing Balloons, they work with important quantitative assumptions about the phenomenon to develop a theoretical model that can predict an appropriate amount of the drug to administer for a particular interval of time.

The activity states the problem as follows:

Suppose that a drug company has established that a patient must have 40 mg of a certain prescription drug in the body for the drug to be effective. Moreover, the company's studies indicate that anything in excess of 600 mg is toxic, and its research has shown that the body eliminates 10 percent of the drug every four hours.

Imagine that you are a doctor prescribing this drug for a patient. How often would you want your patient to take the drug, and in what quantity, to ensure effectiveness while avoiding toxicity?

pp. 93–94; 95–96

Students can use the applet Drug Dosage on the accompanying CD-ROM to investigate dosage problems in which the decrease in the quantity of the drug in the body from one point in time to the next is roughly proportional to the quantity that was present at the earlier time.

The drug dosage problem in Healthy Dose is similar to numerous problems in books on modeling, including *Mathematics Methods and Modeling for Today's Classroom* (Dossey et al. 2002).

Note that the gap between effectiveness (40 mg) and toxicity (600 mg) is large enough to give room for numerous solutions based on varied assumptions.

Depending on the level of your students, you can structure their exploration of this problem in different ways. Advanced students, especially those who are adept at using electronic spreadsheets, will probably be able to solve the problem without much guidance from you. Students who are less skilled, however, will need more direction. You must decide how much, or how little, instruction your students are likely to need.

The drug dosage problem belongs to a large class of problems related to exponential decay and growth. The abundance of these problems reflects the fact that many contexts exist in which the amount of change in a quantity in a certain interval of time is roughly proportional to the quantity present at the beginning of the interval. Thus, whether we are considering the rebound heights of a bouncing ball, the temperature of a cooling object, the unfettered spread of a disease, or the growth of an investment through payments of interest, we can use proportional reasoning to construct a mathematical model. Proportional reasoning provides a useful modeling strategy for connecting mathematics to diverse real-world phenomena.

The CD-ROM that accompanies this book includes an article, "Drug Levels and Difference Equations" (Acker 2004), which presents a series of activities that are similar to Healthy Dose. In these activities, students researched an oral, over-the-counter medication and used difference equations to model blood levels over time in patients taking the drug. Laurent (2005; also available on the CD-ROM) raises an important question about the activities that Acker (2004) discusses. Laurent notes that the modeling in the activities assumes that the body immediately absorbs an entire oral dose of a medication. She remarks that though this assumption is valid for intravenous drugs, the situation is more complicated for oral doses: "Only a fraction of an oral dose is absorbed into the bloodstream; the remainder may be broken down by the stomach and eliminated before it enters the bloodstream" (p. 86). Oral drugs vary in how quickly or completely they are absorbed, and mathematical models often make simplifying assumptions. To make the model in Healthy Dose, the students assume that the oral drug in question is absorbed quickly and entirely into the bloodstream.

In the drug dosage problem in Healthy Dose, the change in the amount of the drug present in a patient's body between time t and time $t + 4$—four hours later—assuming that the patient takes no additional doses, is proportional to the amount of drug that was present at time t. It is very important for students to understand the role that proportionality plays in the problem.

If students lack adequate experience with proportional reasoning, the applet Drug Dosage might provide a useful warm-up. The applet highlights the proportional aspect of the situation. Students can explore examples in which they discover that the decrease in a quantity from one iteration to the next is approximately proportional to the amount of the quantity present at the earlier iteration. The applet does not give the students the percentage of the decrease in the quantity of the drug in the body over time. Nor does it tell them that the change over an

The modeling in Healthy Dose assumes that the patient's body immediately absorbs an entire oral dose of the prescription drug in question. This assumption is valid for intravenous drugs, which enter the bloodstream directly, but oral drugs are absorbed more slowly and less completely. In Healthy Dose, the students assume that the oral drug in question is absorbed quickly and completely into the bloodstream.

interval of time is proportional to the amount of the drug that was present at the beginning of the interval. Instead, the students gain these insights on their own as they work with the phenomenon and try to model its changes.

Part 1—"Experimenting with a Dosage"

Students may at first find the complexity of the drug dosage problem overwhelming. They know that a patient must have at least 40 milligrams of the drug in the body at all times, without exceeding 600 milligrams. They understand that once a patient ingests a dose of the drug, his or her body will begin to work to eliminate it. However, they also know that the patient will be taking additional doses, and the drug would seem to accumulate in the patient's body over time. When students try to put all this information together, they may think, in the words of one student, "There is just too much going on!"

To simplify the situation for your students as they work on part 1, encourage them to focus initially on one dose of the drug. Because the level of the drug must exceed 40 milligrams, they should obviously choose a dose greater than this amount. For instance, suppose a student starts with a dose of 100 milligrams. Table 1.2 is like the one that the students complete in number 1 on the activity sheet "Experimenting with a Dosage." Working from a starting dose of 100 milligrams, the students would fill in the numbers shown for the amounts of the drug remaining in the body at the end of each four-hour interval over the course of a twenty-four-hour period.

Table 1.2.
The Amount of 100 mg of a Drug That Remains in a Patient's Body at the End of Successive Four-Hour Intervals in a Twenty-four-Hour Period

Time (hr)	Amount of Drug in the Body (mg)
0	100
4	90
8	81
12	72.9
16	65.61
20	59.049
24	53.1441

Your students can use arithmetic to complete the table. However, if they are skillful with spreadsheet technology, using an electronic spreadsheet can facilitate algebraic thinking. The spreadsheet can allow them to approach the task of completing the chart with recursive functions, for example. In figure 1.6, column A represents the time elapsed (in hours) since the patient took 100 milligrams of the drug, and column B represents the amount of the drug (in milligrams) remaining in the body at that time. The students should enter the initial amount, 100 mg, in cell **B1** and define a function in **B2** so that the amount in **B2** is 90 percent of the amount in **B1** (since 10 percent is removed every four hours). Likewise, they should define **B3** to be 90 percent of **B2**, and so forth. This step might offer a good opportunity to review the drag-and-fill capabilities that spreadsheets offer for entering formulas quickly in each row.

Another way to use a spreadsheet to complete the chart is to create a function that relates the amount of the drug to the elapsed time. Once students have discovered an algebraic representation, they can enter the function into the spreadsheet and check the resulting data against the data in a spreadsheet set up like figure 1.6. The amount of the drug remaining in the body after four hours is 90 percent of the initial amount, or 0.90×100 mg. The amount at the eight-hour mark is 90 percent of the amount at the four-hour mark, or $0.90 \times (0.90 \times 100) = 0.90^2 \times 100$ mg. Likewise, the amount remaining after 12 hours is $0.90^3 \times 100$ mg. In general, the amount remaining after t hours is given by the expression $0.90^{t/4} \times 100$ mg.

When the students have arrived at this conclusion, they can enter the time in column A of a spreadsheet and define cell **B1** as **0.90^(A1/4)*100.** Then they will be set to determine the remaining values of the table by using the drag-and-fill feature of the spreadsheet.

Alternatively, if your students are more familiar with a graphing calculator than with spreadsheet software, they can use the calculator's sequence capabilities, with **u(0) = 100** and **u(n) = 0.9 u(n–1)**. With either approach, they are applying a function that is recursive, since they are defining each cell in terms of the preceding one.

Part 2—"Fine-Tuning a Dosage and a Schedule"

Part 2 of the activity encourages the students to consider the impact of additional doses on a patient taking the drug from part 1. An initial dose of 100 milligrams allows the patient to maintain an effective level of the drug (at least 40 mg) for an entire twenty-four-hour period. The frequency with which a patient must take doses of a drug is an important consideration in the world of medicine. In the case of the drug in Healthy Dose, a doctor could certainly prescribe smaller, more frequent doses. Doing so might not be practical, however. For example, if the doctor directed the patient to take a dose every hour, the patient might get no sleep!

In part 2, the students select an appropriate dose and consider a timetable for a patient taking the drug—first for a period of forty-eight hours, then for one week, and then for an indefinite period of time. Although the students could create algebraic representations of the situation, they can also apply empirical techniques by using spreadsheet software. Electronic spreadsheets offer a highly effective way to complete the task. A student who was successful in part 1 with a 100-milligram dose might opt in part 2 to recommend that a patient take 100 milligrams every 24 hours. The student could then use a spreadsheet and formulas to complete a chart like that on the activity sheet. The spreadsheet in figure 1.7 shows a shortened version of such a chart.

Fig. **1.6.**

A spreadsheet representing drug levels, at four-hour intervals, in the body of a patient who takes 100 mg of a drug, with the body eliminating 10 percent of the drug every four hours

	A	B
1	0	100
2	= A1+4	= 0.9*B1
3	= A2+4	= 0.9*B2
4	= A3+4	= 0.9*B3
5	= A4+4	= 0.9*B4

	A	B	C
1	0	100	= B1
2	4	0	= 0.9*C1 + B2
3	8	0	= 0.9*C2 + B3
4	12	0	= 0.9*C3 + B4
5	16	0	= 0.9*C4 + B5
6	20	0	= 0.9*C5 + B6
7	24	100	= 0.9*C6 + B7
8	28	0	= 0.9*C7 + B8

Fig. **1.7.**

A spreadsheet representing drug levels in the body of a patient taking a 100-mg dose of the drug every twenty-four hours

In the spreadsheet in figure 1.7, column A represents the time in hours after the initial dose, column B represents the dose that the patient takes at each four-hour interval, and column C represents the amount of drug that remains in the body at the time in column A. Column C shows a recursive formula that gives the values for these amounts as the sum of the amount of the drug remaining in the patient's body from the previous four-hour period and the amount of any new dose that the patient takes.

Students who are skillful with graphing calculators can use the sequence options to create a data table on their calculators. Setting up the table on the calculator would involve reasoning like the following: If n stands for the number of the four-hour interval in the table and the patient takes a dose every twenty-four hours, then he or she takes doses when $n = 1, 7, 13$, and so on. These are the values of n that are congruent to 1 modulo 6, or the values of n that have a remainder of 1 when divided by 6. The fact that there are six four-hour periods between doses indicates that the patient takes a dose every 24 hours.

Representing this situation in a table on a graphing calculator requires calculating the remainder of $(n - 1) \div 6$. On some calculators, the command **mod(n–1,6)** or the command **remain(n–1,6)** gives this remainder. On calculators without these options, the operation **(n – 1) – 6·Int((n – 1)/6)** gives the remainder of $(n - 1) \div 6$. If the remainder is 0 when $n - 1$ is divided by 6, then the table's second column, representing drug dose, should show 100 to indicate that it is time for the patient to take a 100-milligram dose. Otherwise, the second column should show 0. The following function does this if we store **{100, 0, 0, 0, 0, 0}** in list **L1: u(0) = 100** and

$$\textbf{u}(n) = \textbf{0.9 u}(n - 1) + \textbf{L1}[1 + (n - 1) - 6 \cdot \textbf{Int}((n - 1)/6)].$$

Thus, the dosage for every four-hour interval is 0 unless $n - 1$ is a multiple of 6.

Figure 1.8 shows the graph of this function. The plot represents the data for the first ten days in which the patient takes one 100-milligram dose every twenty-four hours. On the basis of this graph, it appears that a daily dose of 100 milligrams will maintain the patient's drug level well above the effective level, yet well below the toxic level.

Students may create a graph like that in figure 1.8 and offer it in support of their conclusions about the long-term safety and effectiveness of the dosage that they are recommending. In the case of a 100-milligram dose, the daily peaks in the graph suggest that the amount of the drug in the patient's body is increasing, but the curvature of the daily peaks also suggests that the size of the increase for each day is declining. The students can use the technology to observe that, after 20 days, the drug amount increases by less than 0.001 milligrams per day. At such a rate, the patient would have to continue to take the drug for more than a thousand years for it to reach the level of toxicity in his or her body!

Such an argument rests on the diagram and thus is quite informal, but students can make a rigorous argument by using the fact, established in part 1, that the body retains about 53 percent of a dose of the drug at the end of a twenty-four-hour period. Thus, students can calculate the daily peaks by the difference equation $P_n = 0.53P_{n-1} + 100$, where n is the number of the day. Combining this equation with

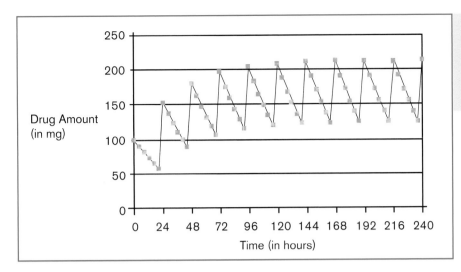

Fig. **1.8.**

Drug levels at four-hour intervals in the body of a patient taking one 100-mg dose of a drug every twenty-four hours for a ten-day period

$P_{n+1} = 0.53P_n + 100$, we get $P_{n+1} - P_n = 0.53(P_n - P_{n-1})$, which establishes the fact that the amount of increase at a given stage is barely half the size of the increase at the previous stage. In other words, the amount of increase each day is getting smaller; in fact, it goes down by almost 50 percent each day.

By the same token, students can argue that the daily minimums remain above the threshold of 40 milligrams necessary for the drug to be effective. Since the maximum values are increasing each day and the daily minimum is 53 percent of the daily maximum, the daily minimums are also increasing, as suggested by the graph. Therefore, if a patient takes a 100-milligram dose of the drug once every twenty-four hours, the amount of the drug in his or her body will always be more than 53 milligrams. With the help of technology, students who choose a once-a-day dose of 100 milligrams can conclude that the level of drug in a patient's body after 20 days will fluctuate between 113 and 214 milligrams.

More advanced students can determine the equilibrium values of the dynamic system $P_0 = 100$, $P_n = 0.53P_{n-1} + 100$. At equilibrium, $P_n = P_{n-1}$. Therefore, by solving $P = .053P + 100$, students will get $P \approx 213$ milligrams as the equilibrium point for the daily peaks for a patient taking a 100-milligram dose every twenty-four hours. This is the value that the peaks are approaching in the graph in figure 1.8.

Assessment

It is important for students to reflect on all aspects of their solutions. When your students have completed part 1, you can assess their progress by orchestrating a discussion of the questions on the activity sheet. Look for students who are unable to describe the change in the drug amount recursively or who complete the chart with difficulty.

When your students have completed part 2, ask each group to make tables and graphs that are large enough to be visible in a classroom presentation of their findings. When the students discuss their work, make sure that they are able to interpret their graphs and tables correctly. Check to see that they reach appropriate conclusions about the dynamic process that they are seeking to control.

Modeling activities invite students to connect mathematical concepts and processes with real-world phenomena. It is important for students to deepen their understanding of this connection. You can assess their progress by posing questions about their models or their assumptions about the context. For example, you could ask them to think about the fact that the daily minimum levels in figure 1.8 are well above the "effective" level of 40 milligrams. You could then pose the following questions:

- "Would a lower daily dose be acceptable?"
- "If so, what would the lowest acceptable daily dose be?"
- "What are the advantages and disadvantages of dosing more frequently than once a day? What about twice a day, for example?"

You can also ask students to do the problem again, this time with information from the Internet on a specific drug of their choice.

Where to Go Next in Instruction

By integrating empirical and analytical techniques, the activity Healthy Dose becomes accessible to a wide range of students. The problem prompts students to think about patterns, reason algebraically, and use advanced mathematical ideas—all in a real-world context. It also encourages queries that go beyond mathematics into such biomedical issues as how the body absorbs drugs, how scientists determine the rate at which the body eliminates a drug, and even how hospitals manage the complicated drug schedules of all their patients.

The final activity in this chapter, Nearest Neighbors, illustrates a context in which the modeling does not involve data, functions, or curve fitting. In many contexts, the models that are most appropriate and provide the most powerful connections between mathematics and real-world phenomena are geometric. The activity Nearest Neighbors allows students to investigate one such context.

Numerous Web sites provide information on specific prescription drugs. For example, the Web site http://www.infomed.org/ frames/100drugs/ provides information on the loading doses, maintenance dosages, and half-lives.

Nearest Neighbors

Goals

- Learn about Voronoi diagrams and use them to model real-world phenomena
- Use geometrical reasoning to construct and validate aspects of Voronoi diagrams

Materials and Equipment

For each student—
- A copy of the activity sheet "Scoping Out the Territory"
- A copy of the activity sheet "Voronoi Vantage Points"
- A compass
- A straightedge
- A sheet of grid paper (optional)

For each group of three students (optional)—
- Access to interactive geometric software such as The Geometer's Sketchpad or Cabri Geometry
- A Mira (or an equivalent reflective device) and/or a piece of waxed paper

pp. 97–99; 100

A template for centimeter grid paper is available on the accompanying CD-ROM.

Discussion

Consider the behavior of territorial animals, such as red-winged blackbirds. What do their territories look like when they live very close to one another? In this context, consider boundaries for assigning students sensibly to one school or another within a school district. What are the customary shapes of the resulting regions in a district with several schools?

In this activity, students focus on three essential features of "territories":

1. *Centers* of interest (for example, schools, nests, or dens)
2. *Boundaries* that enclose the centers
3. *Regions* that the boundaries enclose

These three features, in combination with a very simple rule, are the essential elements of mathematical models that have extremely wide applicability. The mathematical representations of the patterns of centers, boundaries, and regions are called Voronoi diagrams after Ukrainian mathematician Georgy Voronoi (1868–1908), who first studied their shapes (see fig. 1.9).

The Voronoi diagrams in Nearest Neighbors show regions according to the following defining rule:

> In the plane, the region that is associated with a given center consists of all the points that are nearer to the given center than to any other center.

This rule is referred to as the *nearest-neighbor rule*. The points that are not associated with a specific region defined according to this rule

A Mira is a small plastic instrument that students can use to create a reflection of a figure and draw its image by looking through the plastic.

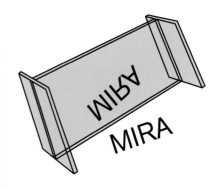

Fig. **1.9.**

Sample Voronoi diagrams

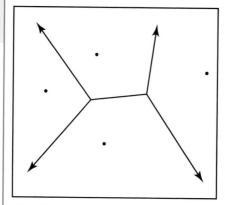 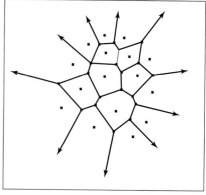

Given *n* points that lie in a plane, we can make a *Voronoi diagram* that partitions the plane into *n* polygons, with each polygon containing exactly one of the *n* points, called a *central point,* and all the points in a polygon being closer to that central point than to any other such point. A Voronoi diagram is also sometimes called a *Dirichlet tessellation,* and Voronoi polygons are sometimes called *Dirichlet regions.*

are called *boundary points,* and any set of centers whose associated regions share a common boundary point are said to be *adjacent centers.* The nearest-neighbor rule is useful for describing animal territories, school-district boundaries, and many other phenomena that are distributed spatially.

The principle underlying the nearest-neighbor rule is *minimization.* In general, when choosing between centers of equal interest, people travel to the center that is closest to them, thereby minimizing their expenditure of time and the other resources necessary for the trip. Likewise, animals will defend the land (or space) that is closer to their home (nest or den, for instance) than to any other similar animal's home, thus minimizing the energy that they must expend in defending territory. By the same token, when there are multiple schools in a school district, the nearest-neighbor rule would suggest that students should attend the school that is closest to where they live, a determination that would minimize the resources necessary for transporting children to and from their homes.

An important geometric theorem underlies the boundaries in the Voronoi diagrams in this activity:

In a plane, the set of all points equidistant from two given points is the perpendicular bisector of the segment determined by the two points.

Part 1—"Scoping Out the Territory"

In part 1 of the activity, students consider different contexts with territorial features and develop scenarios for each one. They reflect on how a school district might draw reasonable attendance boundaries for a group of elementary schools, how animals might map out their territories, and where a hungry pizza lover might choose to go for a pizza.

Once your students have come up with ideas akin to the nearest-neighbor principle, show them a Voronoi diagram like one of those in figure 1.9. Help them articulate a clear statement of the nearest-neighbor rule. Ask them to explain how it represents a defining feature of the diagram.

After helping students develop some understanding of the nearest-neighbor rule, the activity invites them to draw a Voronoi diagram. Then it challenges the students to characterize and define the boundaries that the rule determines. The students may have discovered these boundaries by considering individual test points in the plane and coding them by color or some other system to indicate which animal, school, or pizzeria is most "central" in the context. However, students can think more deeply about the boundaries by deducing an essential truth about them: a point on a boundary will be equidistant from the nearest centers. If need be, you can give them a hint that the boundary points result from a very simple geometric construction—the perpendicular bisector of a line segment.

It should soon become clear that applying the nearest-neighbor rule to a set of centers in the plane produces regions whose edges are the perpendicular bisectors of the line segments joining adjacent centers (see fig. 1.9). Take advantage of the opportunity to review with your students how to use a compass and straightedge to construct the perpendicular bisectors of line segments, as well as other, similar constructions. You might also encourage students to make these constructions with a Mira, waxed paper, or such software for geometric construction as The Geometer's Sketchpad or Cabri Geometry. The Internet also provides construction tools for Voronoi diagrams (see the margin).

Your students will discover that the challenging part of constructing Voronoi diagrams is determining which centers are relevant for a particular boundary. Sometimes the choices are obvious, but at other times they can be perplexing. No matter what construction method the students use, they will not know how far to extend any specific perpendicular bisector until they find the other, relevant perpendicular bisectors that intersect with it. They will probably want to have a good eraser if they are working with pencil and paper. With software such as The Geometer's Sketchpad, they can make liberal use of the "hide" tool to clean up the construction. Regardless of the tools that they use, their completed Voronoi diagrams will show a nonoverlapping set of regions that partition the plane.

It is important for your students to understand that the point of intersection of two or more perpendicular bisectors is equidistant from the endpoints of the bisected segments. In addition, some students are likely to see that that considering three adjacent centers in a Voronoi diagram as the vertices of a triangle lets them discover that the perpendicular bisectors of the segments that the centers determine will intersect at a common point. This point is the *circumcenter* of the triangle. Your students can generalize this insight and prove that any set of three or more adjacent centers will lie on a circle whose center is their common boundary point.

Part 2—Voronoi Vantage Points

Part 2 of Nearest Neighbors is open-ended, inviting students to select and investigate a context that presents a problem whose solution they can model with a Voronoi diagram. The activity sheet suggests a variety of contexts, and you can add to the list or ask your students to brainstorm to come up with other possibilities. Students should choose a context that interests them enough to engage their attention and to be fun to explore.

These sorts of open-ended investigations often turn up interesting questions about the way that animals and humans—as well as inanimate phenomena, such as crystal formations and chemical reactions—partition the space around them. The explorations will be limited only by your students' imaginations. You can have the students work alone or in groups. The activity sheet directs the students to write a report on their

Numerous resources related to Voronoi diagrams are available on the Web. You can find many examples of applications of Voronoi diagrams as well as interesting applets for constructing and exploring such diagrams. The following sites offer a sampling:

• http://www.cs.cornell.edu/ Info/People/chew/Delaunay .html

• http://www.ics.uci.edu/ ~eppstein/junkyard/nn.html

The *circumcenter* of a triangle is the point at which the perpendicular bisectors of the sides of the triangle intersect. It is the center of the triangle's *circumcircle*.

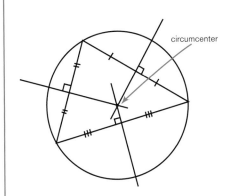

work, but you might decide (instead or in addition) to have them make a poster for presentation to the class. This step can be a very effective culminating activity for the work.

Like the proportionality principle that underlies exponential growth and decay—the central principle in Healthy Dose—the minimization principle that underlies Voronoi diagrams has wide-ranging applications that present many opportunities for connecting mathematics with other disciplines. As your students report on their work, they should include their observations and questions about real phenomena from the context. If they present posters to the class, they should share these ideas. Your students' work in this part of Nearest Neighbors can actualize the full potential of the activity for promoting integrative thinking in the mathematics classroom.

Depending on the level of your students, you can extend their learning from the activity by having them examine the concepts of Voronoi diagrams in the context of coordinate geometry. Tell the students that computer-graphics artists, scientists, and mathematical modelers often use computer programs to construct Voronoi diagrams. At the heart of these programs are formulas for finding equations for perpendicular bisectors and their intersections.

Give your students a sheet of graph paper and the coordinates of a set of four noncollinear points. Ask them to find the equations, including the domains, of the boundaries of the regions of the Voronoi diagram that these points determine. You may even decide that this challenge can serve as an introduction to coordinate geometry, providing you with an opportunity to develop basic skills and ideas.

Assessment

Observation and examination of your students' work in part 2, "Voronoi Vantage Points," can enable you to determine whether or not the students understand the activity's essential principles and geometry at the application level. If you decide to have your students make and present posters, you will have an excellent opportunity to assess their understanding. The posters and presentations should include the elements listed on the activity sheet for a report:

- A complete description of the context and the problem
- A clear statement of the assumptions that the student(s) made in applying a Voronoi model
- A clearly labeled diagram with a brief description of how the student(s) constructed it
- A summary of the evidence that the diagram is useful in describing patterns in the context
- A list of the questions of interest—especially mathematical ones—that have emerged in the modeling process
- A list of real-world constraints that could limit the applicability of the model in specific real-world settings

It is important to have students assess their assumptions in the modeling process. For example, in determining school boundaries, would a Voronoi diagram be appropriate if one school could accommodate twice as many students as another? Would such a diagram be appropriate if the population densities in the areas surrounding schools varied widely? These and other considerations will help students integrate the mathematics with the phenomenon at hand and appreciate the importance and complexity of validating their models.

Conclusion

Like the other activities in chapter 1, Nearest Neighbors illustrates the power of mathematical modeling to connect students' mathematical thinking to arenas outside mathematics. The models in all three of the chapter's activities allow students to apply mathematics very concretely in real-world settings. The principles that underlie each of the mathematical models have wide applicability in other disciplines as well as in mathematics.

Chapter 2 carries these ideas further, investigating some "big" mathematical concepts that extend across students' experiences in the high school curriculum. These overarching concepts provide unifying themes and structures that connect the mathematical topics that students encounter.

NAVIGATING *through* MATHEMATICAL CONNECTIONS

Chapter 2
Connecting with a Unifying Theme

Felix Klein (1849–1925) described geometry, including Euclidean and non-Euclidean varieties, as "the study of those properties of figures that remain invariant under specified groups of transformations." (Boyer 1968, p. 592)

In the Connections Standard, *Principles and Standards for School Mathematics* calls for instructional programs that enable all students to "understand how mathematical ideas interconnect and build on one another to produce a coherent whole" (NCTM 2000, p. 354). One way of accomplishing this goal is to use unifying themes to integrate topics within the main strands of the curriculum. Examples of such themes include set theory, functions, algebraic structure, and graphical approaches to problem representation. Another "big idea"—one that spans topics in algebra, geometry, calculus, and statistics—is transformations. Although students can learn about reflections, translations, rotations, dilations, and scale changes from a purely geometric standpoint, they can apply these notions to the study of functions throughout their mathematical experience, thereby connecting those experiences. Richard Sisley (1995) and others have developed curricular materials that illustrate this potential and that include many detailed examples of the concepts presented in this chapter.

The four activities in the chapter come from different levels and topics in the curriculum for grades 9–12 and illustrate the wide-ranging applicability of transformations. The first activity, Transformers, furnishes a basic introduction. In the activity, students use a graphing calculator to investigate transformations on a geometric figure, which is defined as a locus of points in the Cartesian plane. The students focus on the properties that are preserved by various kinds of transformations. This idea of observing properties that remain unchanged in different contexts is itself ubiquitous in mathematics.

"As students progress through their school mathematics experience, their ability to see the same mathematical structure in seemingly different settings should increase."
(NCTM 2000, p. 65)

The second activity, The Function of Parents, extends the techniques from the first activity and provides a unified approach to studying families of functions. Students then apply these techniques in the third activity, Slinky Transformations, in which they measure the motion of a Slinky spring toy by using a calculator-based laboratory. Finally, in the fourth activity, Line 'Em Up, students gain a better understanding of linear regression in a context that goes beyond merely using the regression feature on the calculator.

Unlike the activities in chapter 1, the activities in chapter 2 do not focus on integrating mathematics with the real world. Rather, they highlight connections among the mathematical tools that students frequently use across the grade levels in their modeling activities. The restructuring phases of modeling and problem-solving processes, illustrated in the introduction to this book, rely on mathematical structures and often use functions to reorganize the information in mathematical representations, allowing problem solvers to draw conclusions. By their very nature, transformations link mathematical structures and thus are an important tool in many modeling and problem-solving activities.

Transformers

Goals

- Introduce translations, reflections, dilations, and scale changes
- Determine invariant properties of transformations

Materials and Equipment

For each student—
- A copy of the activity sheet "Transformers"
- A graphing calculator

pp. 101–4

Discussion

In the activity Transformers, students enter lists of ordered pairs into their graphing calculators and create graphs that consist of line segments whose endpoints are the ordered pairs in the list, connected in the order in which the pairs occur. For example, the graph of the following list of points is a right triangle: {(1, 2), (3, 4), (6, 1), (1, 2)}, as shown in figure 2.1. The activity calls such a list P.

The graph changes when the list of points determining the triangle is transformed into another list of four points. For example, applying the transformation rule ($x' = x + 1$, $y' = y - 5$) to the points in list P, the original list of points, produces the following list, P', of ordered pairs: {(2, –3), (4, –1), (7, –4), (2, –3)}. Figure 2.2 shows the graph determined by P'.

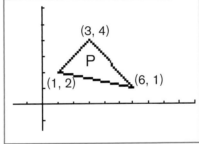

Fig. **2.1.**

A right triangle formed by the graph of the list of points {(1, 2), (3, 4), (6, 1), (1, 2)}, as displayed on a graphing calculator

In figure 2.2, triangles P and P' appear to be congruent. Furthermore, all the points of P appear to have moved the same distance in the same direction. This fact highlights a fundamental insight about the transformation: it "moves" every point in the plane the same distance and in the same direction. Such a transformation is a *translation* of the plane. The lists P and P' provide an indicator of the properties of the transformation. For example, under the translation, any segment in the plane is mapped to a segment that has the same length, and any angle in the plane is mapped to an angle that has the same measure. This activity also introduces students to dilations, scale changes, and reflections in a similar fashion.

The notation $T: P \rightarrow P'$ emphasizes the idea that P is translated to P' in the coordinate plane. Sometimes P' is called the "image of P under the transformation T." The notation that indicates the correspondence between points and their images under the transformation is $T(x, y) = (x', y')$, or, in this example, $T(x, y) = (x + 1, y - 5)$.

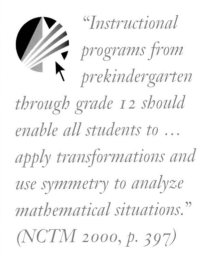

"Instructional programs from prekindergarten through grade 12 should enable all students to ... apply transformations and use symmetry to analyze mathematical situations." (NCTM 2000, p. 397)

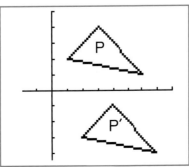

Fig. **2.2.**

Triangle P and its translated image P' as displayed in the ZSquare window of a TI-83 Plus graphing calculator

"In grades 9–12 all students should ...

- *understand and represent translations, reflections, rotations, and dilations of objects in the plane by using sketches, coordinates, vectors, function notation, and matrices;*
- *use various representations to help understand the effects of simple transformations and their compositions."*

(NCTM 2000, p. 397)

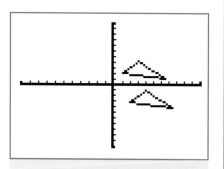

Fig. **2.3.**

Triangle P and its translated image P' as displayed on the ZStandard window of a TI-83 Plus graphing calculator

Thus, $T(0, 0) = (1, -5)$ indicates that $(0, 0)$ is mapped to, or translated to, point $(1, -5)$.

When students use a calculator's window features to study figures, they must be cautious about describing properties that are invariant. Window changes may produce changes that distort the shapes of figures and obscure invariant properties of the transformations. For example, the standard window on a TI-83 Plus calculator distorts the shapes of P and P', since the visual size of a unit in the vertical direction is smaller than the visual size of a unit in the horizontal direction. Compare figure 2.3, which illustrates the effects of the ZStandard window, with the ZSquare window shown in figure 2.2, in which vertical and horizontal units have the same visual length.

Assessment

In the activity Transformers, students need to make sense of the notation used for the transformations. These functions are mappings of ordered pairs to ordered pairs in the plane. The students need to understand that a transformation affects all points in a plane and not just a few points in a select figure of interest. One way to help them focus on this issue is to ask them whether the transformations leave any points fixed, that is, whether the point and its image are the same, or whether any figures are fixed. The translation $T(x, y) = (x + 1, y - 5)$, for example, does not leave any points fixed. However, since this translation moves every point along a path that has slope -5, it leaves some lines fixed. (Every point on a line L with slope -5 is moved to another point on that same line, thereby making the image, L', the same as the original line, L.) Students find that they can more easily determine whether the transformations leave any points fixed when they keep in mind the geometric description of the transformation while they visualize the sets of points that move. In fact, from a geometric point of view, the power of this activity lies in the study of a transformation's effect on the geometric properties of figures.

To assess the students' understanding of the invariant properties of a transformation, ask them to write a journal entry in which they describe and give examples of transformations that preserve angles but not distance, transformations that preserve distances but not angles, transformations that preserve parallel relationships between lines, and so on. Any transformation that preserves distance must also preserve angle. However, $T(x, y) = (2x, 2y)$ preserves angle but not distance. Any transformation that preserves angles must also preserve parallel relations.

Where to Go Next in Instruction

The activity Transformers uses graphing calculators and coordinate representations to provide an introduction to transformational geometry. You can extend the activity to include rotations and compositions of transformations, thereby deepening the students' understanding of transformational geometry. The transformations presented in this activity are examples of *affine transformations* of the type $(x', y') = (ax + by + c, dx + ey + f)$, where a, b, c, d, e, and f are real numbers and $ae - bd \neq 0$. Such transformations are important in the study of geometry.

Linear as well as nonlinear transformations, such as the mapping (breaths, circumference) → ($\sqrt[3]{\text{breaths}}$, circumference) used to linearize the data set in the activity Growing Balloons, can play a large role in curve fitting and in the study of functions in grades 9–12. The following activity, The Function of Parents, illustrates how the geometric transformations introduced in Transformers can be applied in algebraic settings to families of functions.

Navigating through Geometry in Grades 9–12 (Day et al. 2001) includes excellent activities that use transformations in geometry.

The Function of Parents

Goals

- Find equations corresponding to function graphs that have undergone a translation or a scale change
- Learn to use connection diagrams

Materials and Equipment

For each student—

- A copy of the activity sheet "The Function of Parents"
- A graphing calculator

Discussion

Many applications in mathematics involve fitting a function to the graph of a set of points to predict a relationship among the variables represented in the graph. A common strategy is to start with a simple parent function, such as $y = x^2$, and transform it by using such linear transformations as those in the activity Transformers until the resulting function graph closely approximates the graph of the set of points. This strategy has wide applicability in high school mathematics because students can readily obtain the function rule corresponding to the resulting function graph by using the parent function and the transformation rules. This activity, The Function of Parents, helps students develop these transformation skills while deepening their understanding of families of functions.

In the activity, students learn to derive the function rule that describes the ordered pairs in a given graph on the basis of a parent function and the transformations that produce the graph. For example, we can translate the graph of the function $y = x^2$ by using the translation $T(x, y) = (x + 3, y - 2)$. We next consider lists of selected points on the preimage and image graphs, as given in figure 2.4.

pp. 105–8

A number of basic functions, many of which appear on the keypad of the graphing calculator, are sometimes referred to informally as "parent" functions. The function $f(x) = x^2$ is an example of one such function.

Fig. **2.4.**

Lists of selected points on preimage and image graphs of the function $y = x^2$ under the translation $T(x, y) = (x + 3, y - 2)$

Preimage

$P: y = x^2$

x	y
0	0
−1	1
1	1
−2	4
2	4

$T(x, y) = (x + 3, y - 2)$

Image

$P': ?$

x'	y'
3	−2
2	−1
4	−1
1	2
5	2

The question is, What function rule describes the relationship between the coordinates of the image P'? Since the relationship between the x- and y-coordinates of P is $y = x^2$, we can deduce a relationship between the x- and y-coordinates of P'. From $x' = x + 3$ and $y' = y - 2$, we can determine that $x = x' - 3$ and $y = y' + 2$; by substituting these values for x and y into $y = x^2$, we have $y' + 2 = (x' - 3)^2$. When we express this relation in the usual x-y notation, we discover that the equation describing P' is $y + 2 = (x - 3)^2$, or $y = x^2 - 6x + 7$. Figure 2.5 shows the graphs of $y = x^2$ and $y = x^2 - 6x + 7$, along with the points given in the lists.

The preceding example illustrates the steps for finding the function rules for graphs that result from a linear transformation:

Step 1: Solve for x and y in terms of x' and y' by using the transformation rule, and substitute the results into the parent function for x and y.

Step 2: Rename x' and y' as x and y to express the final result in the standard way.

The inverse of the translation $T(x, y) = (x + 3, y - 2)$ is the translation $T^{-1}(x, y) = (x - 3, y + 2)$. This inverse is the translation that maps P' back to P. For example,

$$(-2, 4) \in P \xrightarrow{\ T\ } (1, 2) \in P' \text{ and } (1, 2) \in P' \xrightarrow{\ T^{-1}\ } (-2, 4) \in P$$

The two-step method for generating the formula for P' essentially uses $T^{-1}(x, y)$ to determine what to substitute for x and y in step 1. This process makes sense because when (x, y) is a point on P', its image $(x - 3, y + 2)$ under the inverse translation $T^{-1}(x, y)$ lies on P. Therefore, the coordinates of its image, or $(x - 3, y + 2)$, satisfy the equation for P—that is, $y + 2 = (x - 3)^2$.

When multiple transformations are composed to produce a function graph, a "connection diagram" is useful for showing the stages. Suppose that we need an equation for the parabola that has vertex $(3, -6)$ and passes through the point $(9, 1)$. We start with the "parent" parabola $y = x^2$, which has vertex $(0, 0)$ and passes through the point $(1, 1)$. By using a scale change and a translation, we can derive the equation of the desired parabola. Again, notice that the replacements for x and y at each stage are the expressions that appear in the inverse of the transformation. See figure 2.6.

On the target parabola in the figure, the point $(9, 1)$ is six units to the right and seven units up from the vertex $(3, -6)$. The scale change $S(x, y) = (6x, 7y)$ leaves the vertex of the resulting figure fixed at the origin while moving the point $(1, 1)$ six units to the right and seven units up from the origin. The result is a figure that is only a simple translation away from the target parabola.

Number 6 in the activity asks students about properties that are preserved by scale changes and translations. If a quadratic function $y = ax^2 + bx + c$ is transformed by a scale change $S(x, y) = (rx, sy)$, then the resulting function is

$$\frac{y}{s} = a\left(\frac{x}{r}\right)^2 + b\left(\frac{x}{r}\right) + c,$$

or

$$y = \frac{sa}{r^2}x^2 + \frac{sb}{r}x + sc,$$

which is also a quadratic function. Similarly, translations map quadratic functions to quadratic functions.

Fig. **2.5.**

Graphs of P and P'

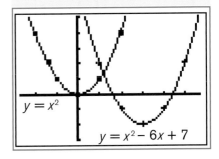

$y = x^2$

$y = x^2 - 6x + 7$

"In grades 9–12, students … should see the interplay of algebra, geometry, statistics, probability, and discrete mathematics and various ways that mathematical phenomena can be represented. Through their high school experiences, they stand to develop deeper understandings of the fundamental mathematical concepts of function and relation, invariance, and transformation."
(NCTM 2000, p. 287)

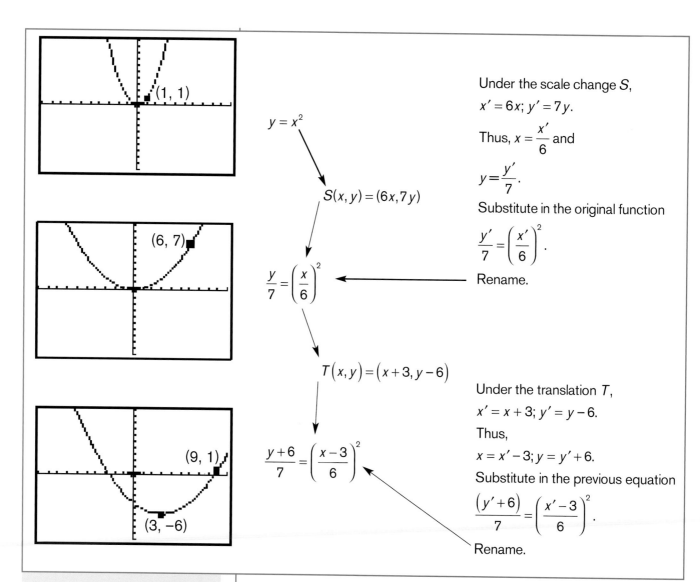

The diagram shows:

$y = x^2$

Under the scale change S,
$x' = 6x; y' = 7y$.

Thus, $x = \dfrac{x'}{6}$ and

$y = \dfrac{y'}{7}$.

Substitute in the original function

$\dfrac{y'}{7} = \left(\dfrac{x'}{6}\right)^2$.

$S(x, y) = (6x, 7y)$

$\dfrac{y}{7} = \left(\dfrac{x}{6}\right)^2$ ←——————— Rename.

$T(x, y) = (x + 3, y - 6)$

Under the translation T,
$x' = x + 3; y' = y - 6$.
Thus,
$x = x' - 3; y = y' + 6$.
Substitute in the previous equation

$\dfrac{(y' + 6)}{7} = \left(\dfrac{x' - 3}{6}\right)^2$.

$\dfrac{y + 6}{7} = \left(\dfrac{x - 3}{6}\right)^2$

Rename.

Points labeled on graphs: (1, 1); (6, 7); (9, 1); (3, −6).

Fig. **2.6.**

A connection diagram mapping $y = x^2$ to a parabola with vertex (3, –6) and passing through point (9, 1)

Assessment

In this activity, students develop basic skills in using a parent function and transformations to generate other functions in the same family. The activity provides several opportunities for observing the students' ability to generate a connection diagram when they derive other functions.

Before students even begin to draw a connection diagram, they must understand sufficient conditions for transforming the parent function to another function in the same x-y coordinate system. When they are transforming the parabolic graph of a quadratic function $y = f(x)$ to the parabolic graph of a function $y = g(x)$, mapping the vertex of $f(x)$ to that of $g(x)$ and mapping one other point of $f(x)$ to one other point of $g(x)$ is sufficient. In a given x-y coordinate system, two points with different x- and y-coordinates determine a unique quadratic function of the form $y = f(x)$ as long as one of the points is designated as the vertex. If a quadratic function $y = f(x)$ has its vertex at (h, k) and if (a, b) is another point on its graph, $a \neq h$ and $b \neq k$, then

$$f(x) = \frac{b - k}{(a - h)^2}(x - h)^2 + k.$$

40

Navigating through Mathematical Connections in Grades 9–12

In the connection diagram of figure 2.5, the point (1, 1) and the vertex (0, 0) of the parent parabola are mapped to the points (9, 1) and (3, –6), respectively, on the target parabola. By using a different set of transformations—for example, a scale change and translation that map the point (2, 4) on the parent parabola to (9, 1) and the vertex (0, 0) of the parent parabola to (3, –6)—students can generate the same target parabola and equation that they previously generated. However, point by point, the correspondences between points on the parent function and points on the target function are entirely different in the two cases. Encourage your students to find alternative transformations for the problems on the activity sheet.

Where to Go Next in Instruction

By using scale changes, dilations, reflections, and translations, students can start with parent functions and generate families of related functions. This activity can extend to many families of functions, including polynomial, rational, trigonometric, exponential, greatest integer, and normal curve functions. Sometimes, however, the target that we are trying to fit is a scatterplot of measurement data rather than a known function belonging to a specific family of functions. The following activity, Slinky Transformations, illustrates how transformations provide useful curve-fitting techniques to generate models for sets of measured data.

Slinky Transformations

Goals

- Use transformations to fit functions to real-world data sets
- Understand sufficient conditions for transforming cosine and sine functions to fit other functions in the family of trigonometric functions

Materials and Equipment

For each student—
- A copy of the activity sheet "Slinky Transformations"
- A graphing calculator

For the class (optional)—
- A motion sensor and a Slinky spring toy, so that the class can gather its own data

Discussion

Many real-world phenomena exhibit behavior that periodic functions can model. Periodic functions are functions that repeat themselves at regular intervals. In grades 9–12, students study the sine and cosine functions, both of which are primary periodic functions with periods of 2π; that is, $\sin x = \sin (x + 2\pi)$, and $\cos x = \cos (x + 2\pi)$, for all x.

Studying such diverse real-world phenomena as the sound waves produced by a tuning fork, the motion of a pendulum, or the variations in the times of sunrise and sunset throughout the year gives students opportunities to use periodic functions in modeling activities. Even though such phenomena are not perfectly periodic in the mathematical sense, periodic functions can serve as useful models for them on restricted domains.

In this activity, students model the motion of a spring. Ideally, the students would generate their own data by using a Slinky spring toy and a motion sensor. However, the activity sheet includes data that students can enter into their calculators if these items are not available or time is limited. We generated the data by placing a motion sensor on the floor and letting a Slinky spring toy oscillate up and down while we held one of the ends of the toy at a fixed height above the sensor. We measured time in seconds and the distances between the motion sensor and the oscillating end of the Slinky spring toy in meters. The students' task is to construct a function that predicts the distance of the Slinky spring toy from the motion sensor as a function of time.

The activity guides students through a sequence of transformations, starting with the cosine function, $y = \cos x$. The first transformation is a scale change to match the apparent period and amplitude of the motion as indicated by the data set. Since the period of the cosine function is 2π, the factor determining the scale change horizontally is the number h such that $2\pi h$ equals the period of the data. Since the amplitude of the cosine function is 1, the factor determining the scale change vertically is the number k such that k times 1 equals the amplitude of the data. After

pp. 109–10

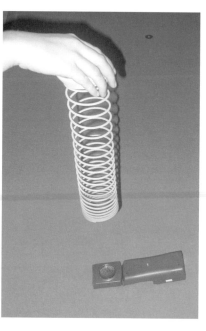

Depending on the resources and time that you have available, your students can use a Slinky spring toy and a motion detector to generate a set of data for the whole class to use, or groups of students can collect their own data.

the scale change has produced a function with the same shape as the data graph, students need to translate this function horizontally by an amount equal to the *x*-coordinate of one of the relative maxima in the data set and vertically by an amount equal to the distance to the "midline." Students can fine-tune the resulting function by using visual clues from the graph. See figure 2.7.

Fig. **2.7.**

Stages of the transformation process, starting with $y = \cos x$

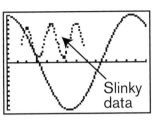

Slinky spring toy scatterplot and $y = \cos x$ graph for $0 \leq x \leq 7, -1 \leq y \leq 1$

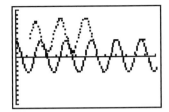

Scale change applied to graph of $y = \cos x$; $0 \leq x \leq 7, -1 \leq y \leq 1$

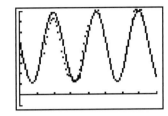

Translation to match graph of function with scatterplot $0 \leq x \leq 4, -0.1 \leq y \leq 0.8$

Depending on the technology available, students can explore many variations of this activity. For example, they can use the Internet to gather temperature data for a year for cities around the world, including some in the Northern Hemisphere and some in the Southern Hemisphere. After students graph the data for a one-year period (twelve data points would be enough to give one cycle), they can transform the sine function to fit their data and compare the functions that they obtain for different cities.

As another variation on this activity, students can gather data produced by measuring the sound waves of various tuning forks with a microphone connected to a calculator-based laboratory. You can challenge them to model the sound waves by transforming the sine or cosine function. The goal is to match the graphs of their transformed functions to the data from the various tuning forks, compare the functions, and discuss how the functions are related to the notes sounded by the tuning forks.

Assessment

In the activity Slinky Transformations, the students need to understand sufficient conditions for determining a periodic function, just as they needed to understand sufficient conditions for determining a parabolic function in The Function of Parents. By picturing one cycle of the parent function and asking how it can be stretched or shrunk in the *x*- and *y*-directions to conform to the data set, the students discover that period and amplitude are critical components in determining the fit.

After the students have completed this activity, you might have them complete the following "identity" project to assess their understanding. Begin by asking the students to transform the cosine function so that it fits the graph of the sine function, $y = \sin x$. Many transformations can accomplish this. The translation $T(x, y) = (x + \pi/2, y)$ generates the function $y = \cos (x - \pi/2)$, whose graph perfectly aligns with that of

$y = \sin x$. It yields the trigonometric identity $\sin x = \cos(x - \pi/2)$. You can then ask the students to transform the function $y = \sin x$ to fit the graph of $y = \sin x \cos x$. A dilation

$$S(x, y) = \left(\frac{1}{2}x, \frac{1}{2}y\right)$$

produces the function

$$y = \frac{1}{2}\sin 2x,$$

which exactly fits the graph of $y = \sin x \cos x$ and illustrates the identity $\sin 2x = 2 \sin x \cos x$.

Finally, ask the students to make a presentation about a trigonometric identity of their choice or one that they discover by using transformations. The presentation should include a discussion of the transformations that graphically illustrate the identity, as well as a proof of the identity by using traditional methods.

Where to Go Next in Instruction

Many graphing calculators allow students to generate sine-function regression equations for sets of data. A good way to extend the activity Slinky Transformations is to ask students to use the sine regression option on their calculators to generate a sine function for the Slinky spring toy data. They can then use their understanding of trigonometry to transform the sine regression function into a cosine function and compare the result with the cosine function that they obtained by using transformations in Slinky Transformations.

Some students might argue that they should have used the sine regression method for fitting the data set in the first place. Such suggestions raise the question of how regression functions on a calculator are obtained. The following activity, Line 'Em Up, shows students how they can generate linear regression equations by using transformations. Such uses of transformations can enhance students' understanding of important mathematical concepts that go beyond the ideas of curve fitting in the previous activities.

Line 'Em Up

Goals

- Use transformations to develop an understanding of how lines of best fit can be calculated for sets of data
- Gain insight into the linear regression option on a graphing calculator by recognizing that the sum of squares of residuals does not change when the data set and function undergo a distance-preserving transformation

Materials and Equipment

For each student—
- A copy of the activity sheet "Sum Squares"
- A copy of the activity sheet "Find the Line"
- A graphing calculator

For each group of three to five students (optional)
- Access to the applet Least Squares (available on the CD-ROM)

pp. 111–13; 114–16

Discussion

Line 'Em Up is appropriate for students who have studied algebra and are familiar with using a graphing calculator for curve fitting. The activity has two parts, "Sum Squares" and "Find the Line."

Part 1—"Sum Squares"

In the first part of Line 'Em Up, students review finding the vertex of a quadratic function of the form $f(x) = ax^2 + bx + c$. The approach in the activity takes advantage of the quadratic formula and ideas about transformations. Students rediscover that the x-coordinate of the vertex is $-b/2a$. They then apply this concept to several problems that involve the sums of squares of residuals.

There are much easier ways to find the vertex of a parabola. For example, if we use the symmetry of the parabola and we find $h \neq 0$ such that $f(h) = f(0)$, then the x-coordinate of the vertex is

$$\frac{h+0}{2}, \text{ or } \frac{h}{2}.$$

Thus, assuming $h \neq 0$,

$$ah^2 + bh + c = a(0)^2 + b(0) + c.$$

This expression simplifies to

$$ah^2 + bh = 0.$$

Dividing by h and then solving for h yield

$$ah + b = 0$$

$$h = \frac{-b}{a}.$$

Therefore, the x-coordinate of the vertex is $\frac{-b}{2a}$.

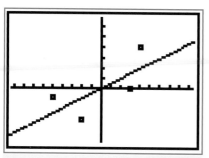

Fig. **2.8.**

The line of best fit through the origin

The use of transformations in Sum Squares helps students see the quadratic formula in a new light. Indeed, by using transformations, one can deduce the quadratic formula without going through the usual method of completing squares.

In "Sum Squares," the students go on to use lines through the origin to estimate the y-values of points in a scatterplot. They find the line through the origin that minimizes the sum of the squares of the residuals. Students can compute the sum of the squares of the residuals by hand, thereby generating a quadratic to minimize. However, the task of generating the sums presents an occasion when students can use a computer algebra system appropriately, especially if they attempt to apply the method to larger data sets. Figure 2.8 shows the line through the origin that is the best fit for the given data set.

Part 2—"Find the Line"

A good way to prepare for part 2 of Line 'Em Up is to allow students to experiment with the applet Least Squares, available on the CD-ROM accompanying this volume. This applet illustrates the idea behind finding the line through a set of data points that minimizes the sum of the squares of the residuals.

In "Find the Line," students seek such a line through a given set of data. They guess a line, compute the sum of the squared residuals, and then compare their results with those obtained by their classmates. They next compute the averages of the x-values ($\bar{x}$) and y-values ($\bar{y}$) of the data set and see how closely the lines that they guessed approach the point $(\bar{x}, \bar{y})$, the *centroid* of the data set. The results should be close enough for the class to agree that the true line of best fit passes through $(\bar{x}, \bar{y})$.

Students then transform the data set by using $T(x, y) = (x - \bar{x}, y - \bar{y})$. This translation moves $(\bar{x}, \bar{y})$ to $(0, 0)$. They should observe that $(0, 0)$ is the centroid of the transformed data set and that translations always map the centroid of a data set to the centroid of its image. Students find the image, under the translation T, of the line that they guessed and compute the sum of the squares of the residuals for this line and the new data set. They should observe that the sum remains the same. Both the preceding observations are valid because translations leave fixed all distance relationships within any figure that is transformed. Such transformations are called *isometries* and include translations, rotations, and reflections of the plane. From these observations, students should conclude that the best-fitting line, L, through $(\bar{x}, \bar{y})$ for the original data set corresponds, under the translation, to the best-fitting line, L', through $(0, 0)$ for the transformed data set.

Because of the design of the data sets, students have already found L' in "Sum Squares." Therefore, to find L, the students translate L' by using the inverse of the original translation—that is, $T^{-1}(x, y) = (x + \bar{x}, y + \bar{y})$. The resulting line, shown in figure 2.9, is the line of best fit under the least squares criterion. When students compare this line with the one that they obtain by using the regression option on their calculators, they need to understand that the roundoff errors that might occur in the computation of $(\bar{x}, \bar{y})$ and in subsequent computations can cause the two lines to differ slightly.

Assessment

This activity guides the students through a single example of finding the line of best fit for a small data set. A good way to assess their understanding is to examine their handling of the last task in "Find the Line." That task gives the students another data set and asks them to use transformations to generate the line of best fit. The students should realize that they made an important assumption in asserting that the line of best fit passes through the point $(\bar{x}, \bar{y})$. Ask the students to explore this assumption by using the linear regression and statistics options on their calculators with data sets that they make up, and have them write an extended journal entry.

A misconception that might result from the activity is the notion that the line of best fit for a data set must pass through the origin. This assumption is true when the origin is the centroid of the data set, but it is not generally true. You can ask students to explain in a journal entry whether the line of best fit of a data set is the same as the line through the origin that is the best fit for the data set. You can also ask them to investigate the conditions under which these lines are the same.

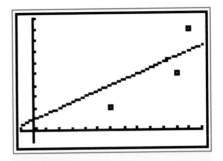

Fig. **2.9.**

The line of best fit $y = 0.5x + 1$

Conclusion

Line 'Em Up is an activity that is appropriate when students begin to apply least squares criteria to the task of finding a function that is the best fit for a set of data. Most teachers refrain from telling their students to learn the formulas for generating linear regressions because the formulas are messy and mysterious to the students. With transformations, however, linear regression does not have to be a "black box" approach to fitting lines to data.

A firm understanding of linear regression prepares students to make sense of other regression options on their calculators. Several regression options available on calculators are not true regressions, since they do not mathematically minimize the sum of squares of residuals. Instead, they provide only approximations to the true regression formulas. For example, the power and exponential regressions on calculators are actually generated by a data transformation, followed by a linear regression on the transformed data, followed by the inverse of the data transformation. Line 'Em Up uses this strategy. Thus, the idea of transformations, beginning with transformations of geometric figures in the plane as in the activity Transformers, can be elaborated and applied in numerous settings throughout the students' entire study of mathematics in grades 9–12 and beyond.

Such unifying themes as transformations provide common tools for establishing relationships within diverse mathematical settings. Because of their wide applicability, these themes also provide coherence within the topics comprising the mathematics curriculum in grades 9–12. The next chapter focuses on using multiple representations of concepts as a means for integrating mathematics in grades 9–12.

NAVIGATIONS SERIES

GRADES 9–12

NAVIGATING *through* MATHEMATICAL CONNECTIONS

Chapter 3
Connecting with Multiple Representations

"Representations should be treated as essential elements in supporting students' understanding of mathematical concepts and relationships."
(NCTM 2000, p.67)

A deeper and more flexible understanding of an idea arises from activities that connect one or more representations of the idea. One useful framework for connecting various representational strategies, found in "Representations and Translations among Representations in Mathematics Learning and Problem Solving" (Lesh, Post, and Behr 1987), is depicted in figure 3.1.

Representation is a process of mathematics that provides an important way to integrate and connect ideas. By naming Representation as one of the ten Standards, *Principles and Standards for School Mathematics* (NCTM 2000) emphasizes the prominent role that the process of representation plays in teaching and learning mathematics. Since thinking and communicating are impossible without some form of representation, it is not surprising that *Principles and Standards* emphasizes the value of multiple representations in learning mathematics. Mathematics textbooks often present ideas and prescribe student work in a single representational mode but pay minimal attention to other possibilities. In this chapter, we provide examples that describe how to develop mathematical understanding by helping students take advantage of the perspectives that various representational modes make possible (see fig. 3.1).

Mathematics—both conceptual and procedural—is widely applicable in different settings because it is abstract. For example, a strong symbolic understanding of exponential functions allows us to represent and solve problems efficiently in many different realms, including finance, population ecology, and radioactive decay. Similarly, an understanding of the rules for the algebraic manipulation of constants, parameters, variables, and equations is a prerequisite for almost all of higher mathematics.

Although mathematics derives much of its power from its abstractness, the development of students' understanding of the nature of mathematics can be a slow process. In presenting mathematical ideas, teachers sometimes leap to the abstract symbolic representation, leaving students behind and reducing the flexibility of their understanding. A rigid

Fig. **3.1.**

Five modes of representation; adapted with permission from Lesh, Post, and Behr (1987, p. 34)

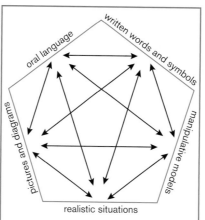

Fig. **3.1.**

Five modes of representation; adapted with permission from Lesh, Post, and Behr (1987, p. 34)

The National Research Council (NRC) highlights the roles that representation and analogy play in developing a stable, yet flexible understanding in *How People Learn: Brain, Mind, Experience, and School* (NRC 2000), a summary of what research on learning has to offer the practice of teaching.

A central theme of Principles and Standards *(NCTM 2000) is connections. Students develop a much richer understanding of mathematics and its applications when they can view the same phenomenon from multiple mathematical perspectives.*

The activity Measurement in the Round is based on "The Wrapping Function Kit" (Kalman 1978), and is similar to activities in various curricula for grades 9–12, including "Can It" (Systemic Initiative for Montana Mathematics and Science [SIMMS] 2003).

understanding is unlikely to facilitate students' transfer or application of knowledge from one domain to another. However, representation and analogy can be important aids in developing a flexible understanding.

We should remember the student's perspective. Such common phrases as "a picture is worth a thousand words" and "let me get a feel for this" point to the value of using multiple approaches in forming and working with ideas, as does the ancient Chinese proverb, "Tell me, I forget; show me, I remember; involve me, I understand." Students who process ideas in ways that are primarily verbal, visual, kinesthetic, or narrative (relating ideas to stories about the world around them) can use these other modes as stepping-stones to the formal representations of most of their mathematical work. Using multiple approaches to develop mathematical representations increases the possibility that a wider range of students can attain a better understanding of even the most abstract and complex mathematical ideas.

One strategy for incorporating multiple representations is to present students with information, ideas, and problems in one mode (for example, a realistic situation or a manipulative model) and ask them to generate and present their work in another mode (for example, a visual or symbolic representation). Another method is to present the same ideas in different representational modes and explicitly connect the modes to show students how the symbolic representation underlies each of them. The three activities in this chapter provide a few examples of these strategies for integrating mathematics by connecting representational modes.

The primary objective of Tiles in a Row, the first activity in this chapter, is to help students gain a better understanding of algebraic formulas by beginning with a problem that emphasizes a visual representation. An added benefit of this task is that it helps students who initially seek a realistic context in making sense of a problem. Tiles in a Row is an extension of the activity Tiling Tubs in *Navigating through Algebra in Grades 6–8* (Friel, Rachlin, and Doyle 2001). Tiles in a Row offers students in grades 9–12 more complicated patterns to represent and places greater emphasis on using algebra to prove the equivalence of different representations.

In the second activity, Measurement in the Round, students manipulate a physical model to gain insight into radians and to learn the role of the unit circle in graphing trigonometric functions. Although teachers who know the topic well might believe that using a can and a strip of paper is unnecessary, a simple activity of this type can help a kinesthetically inclined student achieve a better understanding of radians and trigonometric functions.

The final activity, Transit Graphs, introduces students to a realistic problem that they model, study, and solve by combining multiple graphs into a single visual representation. This technique of combining representations has many applications in the mathematics curriculum, but here we focus on a simple use of it that gives added meaning to linear relationships in a Cartesian coordinate system.

For a nice discussion of transit graphs and the context of the activity Transit Graphs, see "Increasing the Shipping Capacity of the Suez Canal" (Griffiths and Hassan 1978).

Tiles in a Row

Goals

- Connect the meaning of a symbolic expression with a geometric diagram
- Understand equivalent algebraic expressions corresponding to different strategies for counting the same set of objects

p. 117

A template for centimeter grid paper is available on the accompanying CD-ROM.

Materials and Equipment

For each student—
- A copy of the activity sheet "Tiles in a Row"
- One or two sheets of grid paper

Discussion

This activity is designed for a beginning algebra class. Before students can use algebra to model real situations, they need to establish appropriate connections between their symbols and the phenomenon in question. Many students find it easier to make the connection when the context is visual. The purpose of this activity is to provide students with experiences that connect symbolic expressions with visual images. Students find patterns in determining the number of colored tiles that enclose various numbers of white square tiles in a mosaic. The activity encourages students to use many different ways to organize and represent the patterns that they discover. The ideas of algebraic equivalence help them reconcile the different representations of the same counts.

Begin the lesson by asking your students to complete the activity sheet. Working in groups will make it easy for them to do so. After all the students have completed number 3, ask various groups to present their method of counting to the class. To ensure that the students are making a connection between the visual and verbal representations, have them illustrate each method with a diagram.

After your students have presented several methods, choose one and help the class describe it by using a variable such as N to represent the number of white tiles. One method is to count the eight colored tiles around the left, top, and bottom of each white square, as in figure 3.2a. By counting the eight colored tiles for each of the N white squares and the four colored tiles needed to close off the right end of the design, the students discover that the formula for the number of colored tiles is $8N + 4$. Another method is to count the number of colored tiles on top, as shown in figure 3.2b. The students then find that three colored tiles are needed for each white square tile and an additional colored tile is needed on the end: $(3N + 1)$. They must then double that amount to account for the colored tiles on the bottom: $2(3N + 1)$. By adding the two uncounted tiles that lie in each of the $N + 1$ vertical columns, they obtain an answer of $2(3N + 1) + 2(N + 1)$ colored tiles.

This activity is based on "The Wrapping Function Kit" (Kalman 1978).

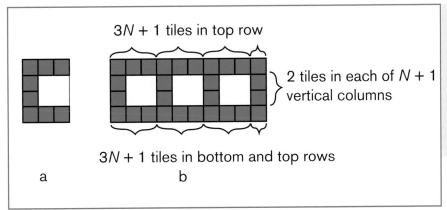

3N + 1 tiles in top row

2 tiles in each of N + 1 vertical columns

3N + 1 tiles in bottom and top rows

a   b

Fig. **3.2.**

Two strategies for counting the colored tiles surrounding N white tiles: (a) counting the 8 colored tiles above, below, and to the left of each white square (and multiplying by N and then adding 4 tiles to finish the pattern on the right), and (b) counting 3N + 1 tiles in the top row, 3N + 1 tiles in the bottom row, and 2 tiles in N + 1 columns

After students have used a variable to describe one or two methods, ask them to work in groups to describe other methods in terms of N. Challenge them to identify two different algebraic expressions for the number of colored tiles and prove their equivalence by using diagrams and algebraic methods. Ask the students to compare how different expressions count the same parts of the diagram in different ways. For example, in the method that is based on figure 3.2a, the eight colored tiles for each of the N white squares contribute three to the top row, three to the bottom row, and one vertical column of two tiles: $8N + 4 = (3N + 3N + 2N) + 4$. The four colored tiles used to complete the design contribute one tile to the top row, one to the bottom row, and one column of two colored tiles: $8N + 4 = (3N + 1) + (3N + 1) + 2(N + 1)$. Combining the expressions for the top and bottom rows yields the expression found by using the second method: $2(3N + 1) + 2(N + 1)$. This discussion offers an opportunity to demonstrate the efficiency of algebraic methods for proving that expressions are equivalent.

Assessment

While the students are completing the activity sheet, circulate to make sure that they understand what the steps of the activity are asking them to do and that they can articulate their methods. To assess the skills and understandings targeted by this activity and to give your students more practice in making connections between symbolic and visual representations, present them with the geometric patterns shown in figures 3.3 and 3.4. Ask them to find formulas for the number of colored tiles in the Nth stage of the patterns in the two figures. Alternatively, you can ask your students to invent different geometric patterns that grow in stages and to find equations for their own patterns. Students can do this assignment as homework or in class. In addition, they can find equations for situations created by other students.

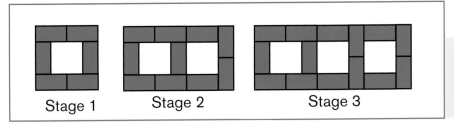

Stage 1   Stage 2   Stage 3

Fig. **3.3.**

The first three stages of a "straight" geometric pattern of tiles, with colored tiles surrounding the white tiles

Fig. **3.4.**

The first three stages of a "stair-stepping"
geometric pattern of tiles, with colored
tiles surrounding white tiles

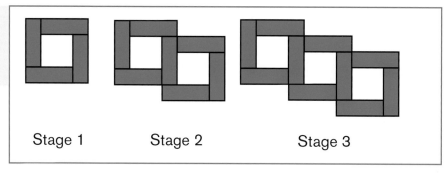

Stage 1   Stage 2   Stage 3

Where to Go Next in Instruction

Tiles in a Row asks students to represent a process of counting tiles
by using visual, oral, and algebraic modes of representation and to
translate among the various modes. The multiple approaches help students make sense of algebra as a language for modeling quantitative
processes and as a tool for establishing the equivalence of different
processes. In the next activity, Measurement in the Round, students
construct a concrete model for the basic concepts of trigonometry. The
activity illustrates how the process of translating abstract ideas into concrete representations can lead to a deeper understanding of these
abstract ideas and their foundations in geometry.

Measurement in the Round

Goals

- Understand radian measure and circular trigonometric functions through a concrete representation
- Review topics in geometry, including circles, central angles, and arcs

Materials and Equipment

For each student—
- A copy of the activity sheet "Constructing a Tape"
- A copy of the activity sheet "Measuring Angles"
- A copy of the activity sheet "Graphing Circular Functions"
- One or two sheets of grid paper

For each group of two to four students—
- A can (for example, a coffee can about 15 cm in diameter; you may wish to give cans with different diameters to each group of students)
- A strip of paper, ribbon, or bias tape (available in fabric stores) with a length that is approximately twice the circumference of the can
- A compass and a straightedge

For the class—
- Overhead transparencies from the blackline master "Defining Trigonometric Functions" (or paper copies for each student)

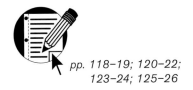

pp. 118–19; 120–22; 123–24; 125–26

A template for centimeter grid paper is available on the accompanying CD-ROM.

Discussion

The activity Measurement in the Round consists of three inter-related parts: "Constructing a Tape," "Measuring Angles," and "Graphing Circular Functions." The concepts of radian measure and the circular trigonometric functions (the "wrapping functions") often seem abstract and arbitrary to students. These activities give concrete meanings to the concepts. Moreover, they encourage students to review geometry. You may want to use "Constructing a Tape" and "Measuring Angles" to introduce students to radian measure or deepen their understanding of it and use "Graphing Circular Functions" at a later time.

Part 1—"Constructing a Tape"

Begin part 1, "Constructing a Tape," by giving your students a can, a strip of paper (or another material), and a copy of the activity sheet. Each group will construct a measuring tape whose unit is one radius of the can. This activity is a good one for pairs of students, but if you do not have enough cans, your students can work in groups of three or four.

The students first trace the circumference of the can on a blank sheet of paper and then find the center of the circle that they drew. To locate the center, students might construct the perpendicular bisectors of two

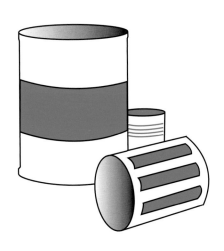

(nonparallel) chords. The center of the circle is the point of intersection of the two perpendicular bisectors. Another method that students might use is to fold the circle onto itself two times, making a different fold line each time. The activity sheet asks students to explain why their method works. The solutions give one possible response.

After finding the center of the circle, the students draw a radius. They can then mark their tape, using that radius as the unit, to begin a measuring tape. Their circle is thus a "unit circle" relative to the measuring tape. The activity ends with a challenge to the students to calibrate their tapes into fifths of the unit. A good extension of this task is to ask students to construct such other numbers on their measuring tapes as 3/4, 4/3, $\sqrt{2}$, or $\sqrt{3}$. The rich geometry that students must use to create a physical representation of a number line without a ruler illustrates the connective power of multiple representational approaches.

Part 2—"Measuring Angles"

After the students have completed their tapes, they can move on to "Measuring Angles," part 2 of the activity. Here the students find angles that have a certain measure in radians. With their tape, they measure an arc of a given size on the unit circle and then draw an angle that subtends the arc. Using this concrete representation helps make the meaning of radian measure come alive.

An angle is the union of two noncollinear rays with a common vertex. Its measure θ is a unique number such that $0 < \theta < 180$ in degrees and $0 < \theta < \pi$ in radians. A *directed angle* is an ordered pair of rays with a common vertex, with one ray designated as the initial side and the other ray as the terminal side of the angle. A directed angle has infinitely many measures, positive and negative, corresponding to the magnitude and direction of all possible rotations of the plane that map the initial side to the terminal side. Measurement in the Round treats angles as directed angles.

Students begin "Measuring Angles" by tracing the circumference of their cans in the center of a blank sheet of paper and constructing *x*- and *y*-axes that intersect at the center of the circle. They mark points on this "unit circle" to indicate different directed angles and use their measuring tapes to measure the corresponding directed arcs, thus finding the "radian" measure for those angles. They then find radian measures for specific arcs on the circle, such as a half-circle or quarter-circle. Though they use cans of different sizes, the students can compare results because they are drawing angles with specific radian measures on their unit circles. Even though the students' circles are of different sizes, the angles that they construct should be approximately congruent.

Physical representations and their comparisons can reveal the deeper connections in abstract concepts. In figure 3.5, the ratio of the arc length of $\overset{\frown}{AB}$ to r_1 is the radian measure of $\overset{\frown}{AB}$ and the ratio of the arc length of $\overset{\frown}{A'B'}$ to r_2 is the radian measure of $\overset{\frown}{A'B'}$. Since $\angle AOB$ and $\angle A'OB'$ are the same angle, these ratios must be the same for radians to be a well-defined measure of directed angles and their corresponding arcs.

Students whose cans are different sizes face this issue when they compare their angle measures. On the basis of their intuitions that all

The article "Irrational Numbers on the Number Line: Perfectly Placed" (Coffey 2001; available on the CD-ROM) explores the possibilities of number-line investigations.

For a similar number-line activity, see Designing a Line in *Navigating through Number and Operations in Grades 9–12* (Burke et al. 2006).

Fig. **3.5.**

In the two "unit circles," the units are different, but so are the arcs that students measure

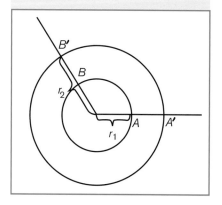

circles are similar or that the circumference is proportional to the radius, they can argue that corresponding parts are proportional. Hence, many students will not be surprised that their measurements are the same, even though their measuring tapes use different units. However, if they examine their assumptions of proportionality, the multiple representations of the radian concept can lead them to further investigations of the properties of circles, chords, arcs, and angles.

Part 3—"Graphing Circular Functions"

The third part of Measurement in the Round, "Graphing Circular Functions," gives a concrete representation of the trigonometric functions. The students apply their work from part 2, "Measuring Angles," in which they discovered that their measuring tapes represented not only lengths whose units are the radius of their can but also the radian measures of the various arcs and their corresponding angles on the unit circle. Here they can use their coordinate systems and unit circles from part 2 to represent the sine, cosine, and tangent functions as lengths in their graphs.

Introduce "Graphing Circular Functions" by displaying a transparency of the blackline master "Defining Trigonometric Functions" on an overhead projector or by giving each student a paper copy made from the blackline master. Discuss the definitions as a class, ensuring that your students are able to find the three functions for a given angle. Then ask the students to complete the "Graphing Circular Functions" activity sheet. The students will need grid paper for their work.

When a directed angle's vertex is at the origin and its initial side is on the positive x-axis, the cosine is the x-coordinate of the point of intersection of the angle's terminal side with the unit circle, and the sine is the y-coordinate of the point of intersection of the angle's terminal side with the unit circle. These definitions are the standard ones for the sine and cosine as functions on the entire real line. Students can see this connection by treating their measuring tape as a part of the real number line. By fixing the 0 of their measuring tape at the point $A(1, 0)$ and wrapping the tape around the circle (using their can as a guide if necessary—see fig. 3.6), they establish the correspondence of points on their "real number line" with points on the unit circle. Thus, the cosine of a point on their real number line is the x-coordinate of the corresponding point on the unit circle; the sine of a point on their real number line is the y-coordinate of the corresponding point.

The tangent is usually defined as the ratio of the sine to the cosine. Another definition, however, can make this idea more concrete. It allows students to measure—and not merely calculate—the tangent of an angle. The tangent of an angle whose terminal side intersects the unit circle at

An angle whose terminal side is vertical has a cosine equal to 0. The common definition of the tangent is the ratio of the sine to the cosine. The tangent of such an angle is therefore not defined, since the ratio has denominator 0.

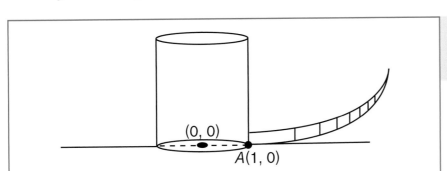

Fig. **3.6.**

Using a can as a guide to wrap the tape around the unit circle

a point B is the y-coordinate of the intersection point of the line $x = 1$ and the line through B that passes through $(0, 0)$. See figure 3.7. The tangent is not defined for angles whose terminal sides are vertical.

Fig. **3.7.**

The tangent of the angle AOB is the y-coordinate of the point of intersection of the line $x = 1$ and the line through B that passes through the origin $(0, 0)$

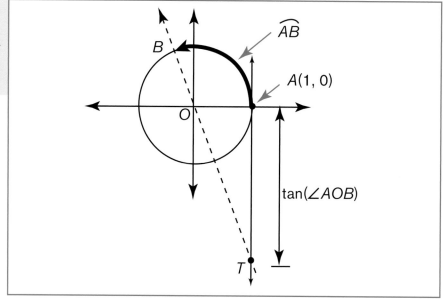

When your students have completed their graphs, ask them to compare their work with that of students who used cans of different sizes. Students should see that all the graphs are similar in shape and that they repeat at intervals of 2π, although their unit distances differ. You might also ask your students to prove that the definition of tangent given in the activity is equivalent to the usual one. They can show this idea by using basic ideas of similar triangles. The triangles shown in figure 3.8 are similar. Hence, the ratios of their corresponding sides are equal.

Using technology can enhance the students' understanding of the definitions of radian measure and trigonometric functions that this activity presents. Many Internet sites contain trigonometry applets that provide dynamic representations for helping students see the bigger picture of the hands-on activity and connect it with the abstract definitions in their textbooks.

Assessment

The activity Measurement in the Round requires students to construct physical representations of several fundamental concepts of trigonometry. When you evaluate the physical constructions that your students have made, you can often spot conceptual difficulties. For example, some students may have trouble understanding how to construct π on their number lines and how to divide a unit length into five equal parts. Other students may have problems understanding how to use the unit circle to find the sine and cosine for points on their x-axis. Also, for values of x close to points where the tangent is not defined, the physical construction may break down if the tangent values are too large in magnitude to fit on the paper that the students are using for their graphs. Pay attention to what your students conclude about the behavior of the tangent function near these x-values.

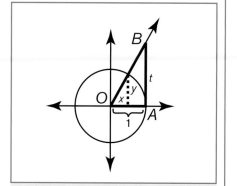

Fig. **3.8.**

$$\text{Tan}(\angle AOB) = \frac{\sin(\angle AOB)}{\cos(\angle AOB)} = \frac{y}{x} = \frac{t}{1} = t$$

Visit Maths Online at http://www.univie.ac.at/future .media/moe/galerie/trig/trig.html for useful dynamic representations of trigonometry.

Giving students an opportunity to compare their results when they are using cans of different sizes is an important part of this activity. The students' discussions can reveal whether they are making the basic connections. For example, they should realize that even though their graphs differ in size because of differences in their unit lengths, the numerical values that the graphs yield for various values of the sine, the cosine, and the tangent are the same.

Where to Go Next in Instruction

Measurement in the Round illustrates the possibilities of developing physical representations for mathematical concepts. Because the various sizes of the cans yield different physical models, students can begin to grasp the generality and wide applicability of the mathematical concepts that the physical models have in common.

The following activity, Transit Graphs, illustrates the rich possibilities of developing mathematical representations for real-world processes. The activity starts with a task from the work world—scheduling the passages of ships through a canal—and leads students to construct a *transit graph*—a novel mathematical representation that brings together familiar mathematical representations. The process of combining commonly taught mathematical representations, such as the graph of a straight line, to form a new representation, such as a transit graph, occurs frequently in mathematical modeling situations. The process not only strengthens students' understanding of the original representations but also helps them appreciate the power that connecting the representations can produce.

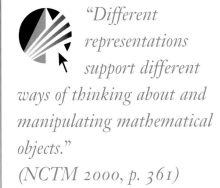

"Different representations support different ways of thinking about and manipulating mathematical objects."
(NCTM 2000, p. 361)

Transit Graphs

Goals

- Introduce a powerful mathematical representation for scheduling problems that involve one-way sections of roads, rails, or canals
- Provide a meaningful context for understanding elementary concepts of a Cartesian coordinate system
- Practice interpreting and creating graphs that depict linear relationships

Materials and Equipment

For each student—
- A copy of the activity sheet "Graphs That Tell Stories"
- A copy of the activity sheet "Creating Optimal Schedules"

For each group of students (optional for assessment)—
- Blank transparencies and markers

For the class—
- Overhead transparencies from the blackline master "Interpreting Transit Graphs"

pp. 127–29; 130–33; 134–35

Discussion

In 1973, the Suez Canal Authority hired mathematicians to study the scheduling of ships through the Suez Canal (Griffiths and Hassan 1978). Throughout most of the north-south length of the Suez Canal, travel must be in one direction because the ships that use the canal are so large. At two places along the canal, lakes and docking facilities permit northbound ships to pull out of the way while southbound ships pass (and vice versa). In studying the problem and creating an optimal schedule, mathematicians used a model that relied fundamentally on transit graphs.

Transit graphs are useful in situations where travel occurs in two directions along the same route but traffic flow on segments of the route must be one-way. Figure 3.9 shows a map of a canal and a transit graph displaying the motion of a northbound ship through the canal. Canals, railroads, mining operations in narrow tunnels, and highway construction present situations that transit graphs can model.

Instead of focusing on the intricacies of complex scheduling problems, this lesson introduces students to the fundamentals of transit graphs in the context of the students' study of the Cartesian coordinate system. As a useful warm-up activity, you might have your students enact the movement of a ship through the canal by moving across the room. You can challenge students who are familiar with motion sensors and calculator-based data-gathering devices to simulate a given ship's trip or to match its transit graph by moving a motion detector.

Draw a map of a fictitious canal and use it in demonstrating that the movement of ships through the canal can be depicted in the Cartesian

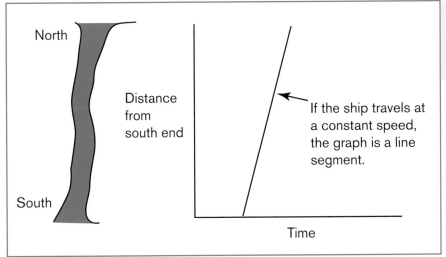

plane if the horizontal axis represents time and the vertical axis represents distance from one end of the canal (see fig. 3.9). Discuss informally with the class several examples of transit graphs. (You can use transparencies that you make from the blackline master "Interpreting Transit Graphs.") Students need to understand the following important concepts of such graphs:

- Slope represents velocity, and positive and negative slopes represent speeds in opposite directions.
- A horizontal line indicates a ship at rest.
- A vertical line is meaningless because a ship cannot be in more than one place at one time and because the velocity (slope) is undefined for vertical lines.
- Although slanted lines appear on the graph, all movement is in fact along the line defined by the canal or a ship's route of travel; the orientation of the segments on the graph does not indicate a ship's movement.

In transit graphs, exact ordered pairs of the form (time, distance) can be calculated by using the following familiar relationship: *distance = rate • time*. This equation is equivalent to $y = m \cdot x$, where m is the velocity of the ship in question. In transit graphs, y-intercepts do not play a big role because positions of ships beyond the ends of the canal are not relevant. (Use the transparencies to work some sample computations.)

Part 1—"Graphs That Tell Stories"

After discussing the ideas of transit graphs with the class, ask the students to complete the activity sheet "Graphs That Tell Stories," part 1 of Transit Graphs, by creating graphs for the scenarios and interpreting the graphs. Encourage the students to compute the coordinates of specific points on their graphs. Being able to find exact coordinates will be useful to the students when they create detailed schedules.

Part 2—"Creating Optimal Schedules"

The second part of the activity involves displaying cyclic schedules on a single transit graph. Most schedules are cyclic, so the scheduler can replicate one complete schedule and then string copies together end to end to represent multiple cycles (for example, days, if the schedule repeats every 24 hours). One transit graph of a complete cycle is enough, however, to represent the slot in the schedule occupied by a ship that begins its trip on one day and ends it on the next.

Figure 3.10a shows a graph of a repeating schedule. A northbound ship enters a canal. As soon as it completes its trip through the canal, a southbound ship enters the canal, and the pattern continues. A scheduler can use the period of the schedule (perhaps 24 hours) to break the long graph into a series of identical shorter graphs, as in figure 3.10b. Finally, the scheduler can isolate a single cycle of the graph, as in figure 3.10c. The scheduler recognizes that this graph applies a technique called *wrapping*, often used in video games, in which anything that disappears off the right edge of the graph reappears at its left edge. Figure 3.10c depicts the schedule of three ships, A, B, and C. Ship A departed the day before ships B and C did; ship C will arrive the day after the day it left (a red-eye trip). From the scheduler's point of view, the two line segments A and C represent one slot in the schedule.

Fig. **3.10.**

A graph of a repeating schedule (distance against time) appears in (a), (b) divides the graph by the period of the cycle, and (c) shows one cycle with segments labeled *A,B,* and *C*. Line segments *A* and *C* represent one slot in the cycle.

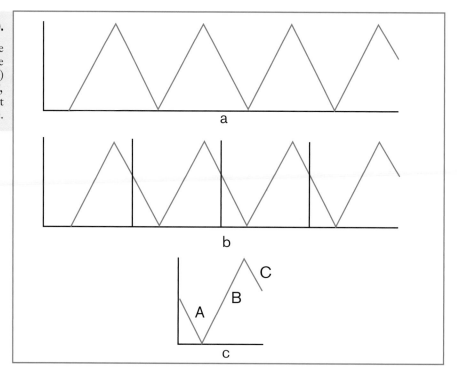

The activity sheet "Creating Optimal Schedules" includes simple scheduling problems that ask the students to assume the following arbitrary parameters: the canal is 50 km long, all ships travel at a rate of 10 km/hr, and the cyclic schedule repeats every 24 hours. Students may gain the following insights through their work on these problems:

- The longer the cycle, the more efficient the schedule; however, ships must wait for longer periods.
- A lot of time is wasted waiting for the last ship in a convoy to leave the canal.
- A bypass zone can help improve a schedule's efficiency.

Assessment

In Transit Graphs, students need to understand how to interpret and construct line graphs that represent uniform linear motion when they are given the velocity and time intervals of the motion. If your students have difficulty interpreting the distance-time graphs, use a motion sensor and ask the students to simulate various motions with constant, as well as changed, velocities and study the resulting distance-time graphs.

When students combine distance-time graphs of many moving objects over the same time interval, they may find the resulting representation very illuminating—if they can keep track of how the various graphs relate to the physical situation.

To assess your students' understanding of the transit graphs with multiple ships, you can discuss various scenarios with them, including asking them to explain what it means when two lines in a transit graph intersect each other. You might pose these situations as prompts for journal entries. Another good way to check the students' understanding is to ask several groups to make transparencies from selected graphs that they produce and have them explain their graphs to the entire class.

Conclusion

In using or in creating multiple representations of mathematical concepts, students learn important ideas about equivalence and make important connections between and within mathematical systems of representation. Chapters 2 and 3 have focused on the connections between mathematical concepts and representations. The next chapter focuses on the integrative habits of mind whose roles *Principles and Standards* emphasizes in leading students to these connections.

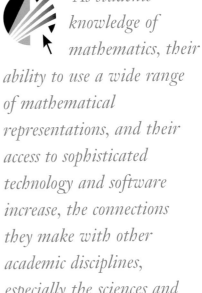

"As students' knowledge of mathematics, their ability to use a wide range of mathematical representations, and their access to sophisticated technology and software increase, the connections they make with other academic disciplines, especially the sciences and social sciences, give them greater mathematical power."
(NCTM 2000, p. 354)

NAVIGATING *through* MATHEMATICAL CONNECTIONS

Chapter 4
Connecting with Problem-Solving Processes

Although curricula tend to separate mathematics into distinct courses, the students benefit when instruction lifts the barriers. To prepare for the interdisciplinary demands of the workplace, students should become accustomed to drawing on any mathematical concepts that they know when they solve problems. This experience occurs naturally in a curriculum that emphasizes the connectedness of mathematical concepts, processes, and representations and their ties to the real world. Such an emphasis makes students more able to draw on appropriate problem-solving tools in new and unfamiliar settings, since they see firsthand how their skills and concepts are applicable in different contexts.

The Curriculum Principle in *Principles and Standards for School Mathematics* (NCTM 2000) emphasizes the importance of a coherent curriculum:

> Mathematics comprises different topical strands, such as algebra and geometry, but the strands are highly interconnected. The interconnections should be displayed prominently in the curriculum and in instructional materials and lessons. A coherent curriculum effectively organizes and integrates important mathematical ideas so that students can see how the ideas build on, or connect with, other ideas, thus enabling them to develop new understandings and skills. (NCTM 2000, p. 15)

In addition, *Principles and Standards* describes how the secondary school curriculum can help students appreciate multiple perspectives:

> One way to have students see mathematics in this way is to use instructional materials that are intentionally designed to weave together different content strands. Another means of achieving content integration is to make sure

that courses oriented toward any particular content area (such as algebra or geometry) contain many integrative problems that draw on a variety of aspects of mathematics, that are solvable using a variety of methods, and that students can access in different ways. (NCTM 2000, p. 289)

The three activities in this chapter present integrative problems that lend themselves to a variety of mathematical approaches. Students approach the problems through empirical investigations, dynamic investigations that draw on technology, and inductive and deductive strategies, as well as by using mathematical tools from the content strands that *Principles and Standards* outlines. However, unless students have developed integrative habits of mind, such problems will not achieve their purpose, whether these problems appear in courses oriented toward particular strands of mathematics or in integrated courses. Therefore, this chapter emphasizes such "connective processes" as thinking back and extending a solution, devising alternative solutions, generalizing, proving, and reasoning by analogy. These connective approaches are important parts of the Process Standards described in *Principles and Standards*.

The problems presented in this chapter are set in real-world contexts that should engage students' imaginations. As with many such problems, they do not belong exclusively to any one of the traditional courses in secondary school but could easily fit into several courses. At the same time, these problems are merely examples of investigations that emerge when connective processes are applied to a basic problem. The solutions lend themselves to progressive elaboration and analysis, reflecting the multifaceted nature of the activities.

The first activity of this chapter, Quick Response Time, offers a geometric setting, but algebra may help students find a solution. The mean and the median, key ideas from data analysis, arise when students investigate different proposals for solving this real-world problem. The second activity, Double-Dare, introduces students to the concept of expected value. The activity invites students to approach the problem first through a simulation and then through the use of an area diagram. The third activity, Support Cables, provides another geometric setting, and students first seek its solution through careful drawings. Students use interactive geometry software to confirm the conjectures that they formed in the drawing activity, and they next prove the result geometrically. Finally, they prove the result by using analytic geometry and generalizing it.

Quick Response Time

Goals

- Explore an optimization situation
- Deepen understanding of median and mean
- Explore and compare distance functions

Materials and Equipment

For each student—
- A copy of the activity sheet "Selecting a Location"
- A copy of the activity sheet "Generalizing Results"
- A copy of the activity sheet "The Fairest of Them All"
- A graphing calculator

pp. 136–38; 139–40; 141–43

Discussion

Mathematics often yields optimal solutions to real-world problems. In this activity, students explore various plausible answers to an optimization problem. The scenario assumes that several small towns are at various mileposts along a rural stretch of highway. The towns have decided to pool their funds to build a fire station. The planners wish to choose the best location along the highway for the station. Students' answers to the problem depend on the criteria that they establish for "best."

The activity has three parts and illustrates how a single problem can be progressively elaborated into an integrative problem by means of basic problem-solving processes. The activity is appropriate for students who have an understanding of algebra and statistics. Students should work in groups of two or three to compare their results and discuss their ideas. Before starting the activity, you should discuss with your students the idea that they can consider the highway in the problem as a number line with some points designated by mileposts and all other points represented by appropriate decimal numbers.

Part 1—"Selecting a Location"

In part 1 of the activity, the "best" location is the point on the highway that minimizes the sum of the distances to the towns. After students experiment with specific locations, they discover that for towns at mileposts 5, 17, and 20, the optimal location appears to be the median of the data set {5, 17, 20}, or milepost 17. Since students cannot test every point between mileposts, they cannot be certain at this stage of the activity that milepost 17 is the best location.

Students extend their result by determining the optimal location for towns at mileposts {0, 5, 17, 20}. In this situation, the station can be located at any point on the segment of highway between milepost 5 and milepost 17. The median again gives an optimal solution. Finally, students consider a case with five towns, at mileposts {0, 5, 17, 20, 23}, and again discover that the median of the mileposts gives the optimal solution.

"Selecting a Location" challenges students to generalize their conclusion for any number of towns along the highway and to provide a convincing argument that the median of the mileposts minimizes the sum of the distances from the fire station to the towns. The students may not be able to answer this question fully at this point, but just considering the challenge is important. The activity also challenges students to consider whether minimizing the sum of the distances is the "fairest" criterion for determining the best location of the fire station. Parts 2 and 3, "Generalizing Results" and "The Fairest of Them All," explore these questions.

Part 2—"Generalizing Results"

In part 2, students represent the sum of the distances from the fire station to the towns as a function of x, the station's milepost. For example, in the case of Littleton, Smallsville, and Tinytown, the distance function is $f(x) = |x - 5| + |x - 17| + |x - 20|$.

After the students have completed number 1, in which they write expressions for the distances from a point x to each of the towns, you should have them pause to discuss their answers as a class. The students should understand that the distances must be positive, and the absolute value function will yield the positive difference between x and the milepost of any town, no matter what x is. The students need the absolute values because they are interested in the magnitude of the distances between the towns and not the directed distances, which could be negative. Figure 4.1 shows the (a) graph of $f(x)$ and (b) a zoomed-in view of the minimum. You might also need to review how to graph an absolute value function on a calculator.

Fig. **4.1.**

A graph of the distance function
$f(x) = |x - 5| + |x - 17| + |x - 20|$,
(a) on a graphing calculator and
(b) with the minimum point revealed by
zooming in

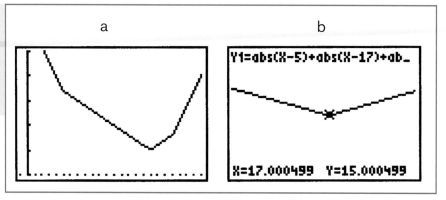

a   b

When the students include a fourth town, Bug Crossing, they must modify their function to $f(x) = |x - 0| + |x - 5| + |x - 17| + |x - 20|$. Figure 4.2 shows the graph of $f(x)$. The minimum occurs over the entire interval between 5 and 17. The students must modify their function again, to $f(x) = |x - 0| + |x - 5| + |x - 17| + |x - 20| + |x - 23|$, when they include a fifth town, Punyberg. The graph supports the idea that its minimum occurs at 17. See figure 4.3.

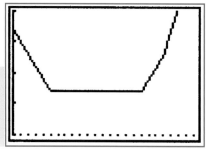

Fig. **4.2.**

A graph of $f(x) =$
$|x - 0| + |x - 5| + |x - 17| + |x - 20|$,
the distance function with four towns

Although the calculator provides compelling evidence that the median minimizes the sum of the distances to the towns, this evidence is not a mathematical proof. Number 7, the final task in part 2, asks only for general conclusions; however, a general argument is possible. The following argument is for a set of five numbers, but it can be adapted to prove the other cases as well:

If $\{x_1, x_2, x_3, x_4, x_5\}$ is a set of real numbers and if $x_1 \leq x_2 \leq x_3 \leq x_4 \leq x_5$, then its median is x_3. If $f(x)$ is the sum of the distances between x and the five real numbers in the set and if $D = f(x_3)$, then we must show that D is the minimum of $f(x)$. To do so, we need to show that $f(x_3 + \in)$ and $f(x_3 - \in)$ are greater than D for any positive value of $\in$. Using a number line is an easy way to show this result. Moving the station a distance of $\in$ to the left of x_3 increases by $\in$ the distance to the station for all points on the right of or equal to x_3 (see fig. 4.4). Since x_3 is the median, these points represent more than half the points in the given set. For the points in the set that are less than x_3, this move decreases the distance to the station by $\in$, at most, if it decreases the distance at all. Since the number of points in the set that are less than x_3 is less than half the number of points in the set, the total decrease in distances does not offset the total increase. Thus, $f(x_3 - \in) > D$.

A similar argument shows that $f(x_3 + \in) > D$.

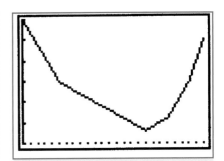

Fig. **4.3.**

A graph of $f(x) = |x - 0| + |x - 5| + |x - 17| + |x - 20| + |x - 23|$, the distance function with five towns

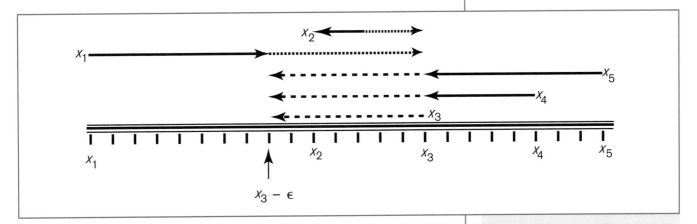

Fig. **4.4.**

Suppose that the fire station is moved from the median x_3 to $x_3 - \in$. Dashed segments represent increases in the distance from a town to the station because of the move. Dotted segments represent decreases resulting from the move. (In the case of x_2, the dotted segment shows the net decrease in the distance to the station.)

Part 3—"The Fairest of Them All"

Part 3 explores proposals by Bug Crossing, Tinytown, and Littleton to change the criterion for the "best" location for the fire station. These towns question the idea that the "best" location is the one that minimizes total distance (and therefore total response time) from the five towns. The citizens of Bug Crossing, Tinytown, and Littleton suggest that the criterion for the "best" location should be "centrality" rather than minimum total distance, and they propose ways of finding a location that is at the "center" of the five towns. In this part of the activity, students should begin to realize that mathematics can help them decide what is optimal when everyone agrees on particular criteria for the best option. In real life, however, politics usually come into play in determining the criteria for the "best."

The citizens of Bug Crossing propose that the spot exactly halfway between Bug Crossing and Punyberg—the towns that are farthest apart on the highway—be recognized as the center and therefore the "fairest" place for the fire station. The citizens of Tinytown contend that the original plan favors the three cities on the east and Bug Crossing's plan favors the two cities on the west. They recommend that the center be

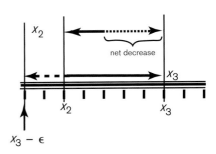

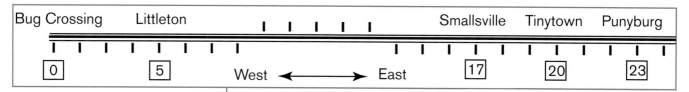

recognized as the point on the highway from which the total of the distances to the cities on the west equals the total of the distances to the cities on the east. The citizens of Littleton propose identifying the center as the point that minimizes the "spread" in the distance data—that is, the point that minimizes the standard deviation of the towns' distances from the fire station. They point out that minimizing the sum of the squares of the distances of the towns to the fire station will give a location that satisfies their criterion.

Two of the proposals in "The Fairest of Them All"—those from Tinytown and Littleton—yield the same result. The citizens of Tinytown want the fire station situated so that the total of its distances to the towns west of it equals the total of its distances to the towns east of it. Mathematically, the *centroid*, or average, of the mileposts of the towns satisfies this criterion. For a set of real numbers $\{x_1, x_2, ..., x_n\}$ with x any real number, $x - x_i$ is positive for all x_i in the set that are less than x and is negative for all x_i in the set that are greater than x. The value of x for which the sum of the negative differences equals the sum of the positive differences is the solution to the equation $(x - x_1) + (x - x_2) + ... + (x - x_n) = 0$. Solving for x gives the result $nx - (x_1 + x_2 + ... + x_n) = 0$. Thus,

$$x = \frac{(x_1 + x_2 + ... + x_n)}{n},$$

which is the mean of the set. If we think of the mileposts of the towns as the set of numbers and, for any location x, we treat the distances of the towns to the west of x as negative and those to the east as positive, then the preceding analysis applies to the problem of placing the fire station.

Littleton's proposal seeks to minimize the square of the distances rather than the total of the distances to all the towns. In number 4 of "Selecting a Location," the students found that minimizing the sum of the distances to the towns leads to choosing a site at the median of the set of town mileposts. The median is not sensitive to outliers; hence Littleton's citizens consider it unfair to their town. Using the median can lead to large deviations in the distances from the towns to the station. For example, calculated as in number 4 of "Selecting a Location," the median would have located the fire station at milepost 17 even if Littleton had been located 100 miles farther west. Littleton's proposal seeks to minimize the standard deviation of the towns' distances from the fire station. Thus, if x is the location of the fire station and x_i represents the location of town i, then the standard deviation from x of a set of n town locations is

$$\sqrt{\frac{\left((x_1 - x)^2 + (x_2 - x)^2 + ... + (x_n - x)^2\right)}{n}}.$$

To minimize the standard deviation, one must find a value of x that minimizes the numerator in the expression—that is, the sum of the squares of the distances from x to the towns. The appropriate value of x is the mean of the x_i.

By using graphs, the students can discover that Littleton's proposal leads to identification of the same location as Tinytown's proposal. However, the result can be proved analytically. If $\{x_1, x_2, \ldots, x_n\}$ is the set of milepost locations of the towns and if x is the location of the station, then the sum of the squares of the distances is $(x - x_1)^2 + (x - x_2)^2 + \ldots + (x - x_n)^2$. Expanding this expression gives $x^2 - 2x_1x + x_1^2 + x^2 - 2x_2x + x_2^2 + \ldots + x^2 - 2x_nx + x_n^2$. Combining like terms yields

$$nx^2 - 2\left(\sum_{i=1}^{n} x_i\right)x + \sum_{i=1}^{n} x_i^2.$$

This quadratic expression is of the form $ax^2 + bx + c$, and the x-value of its minimum is $-b/2a$. Therefore, the optimal value for x, the value that minimizes the sum of the squared differences, is

$$\frac{2\left(\sum_{i=1}^{n} x_i\right)}{2n}, \text{ or } \frac{\sum_{i=1}^{n} x_i}{n},$$

the mean of the set. Students who are familiar with minimizing quadratic functions and using the set of specific mileposts $\{0, 5, 17, 20, 23\}$ can pursue this line of reasoning to prove the result for the situation posed in "The Fairest of Them All."

Assessment

Quick Response Time provides a context in which students must determine the "middle," or "center," of a data set. The students' intuitions will tell them that the towns should locate the fire station near the mean or the median of the data set or at the midrange point, which is halfway between the least and greatest values in a data set. Each of these parameters of the data set corresponds to the optimal solution of one of the proposals for locating the fire station. A good way to assess the students' grasp of the essential ideas is to assign the proposals to different groups. Ask each group to create a poster presentation that outlines the merits of its proposal and uses mathematics to derive the location of the station if the proposal is followed. The poster presentations will provide a forum for discussing the basic ideas of this activity as a class. These presentations will also allow you to assess how students synthesize and extend the results of the activity.

Where to Go Next in Instruction

Quick Response Time illustrates the integrative potential of the problem-solving process in creating extensive connections within mathematics. By considering analogous proposals for solving a real-world problem, your students can make connections that they might otherwise never have made. You can also have your class study analogous contexts. For example, by considering the populations of the various towns, your students can encounter the idea of weighted averages.

Quick Response Time firmly connects mathematical concepts that the students already have encountered, including the mean, the median, and absolute value. The following activity, Double-Dare, illustrates how students can use connective problem-solving processes to discover and develop new concepts.

Double-Dare

Goals

- Understand how to work with an expected-value situation
- Use a simulation, a geometric representation, and an algebraic solution to work with the same problem
- Confirm the findings of a simulation with probability theory

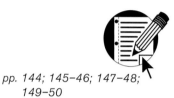

pp. 144; 145–46; 147–48; 149–50

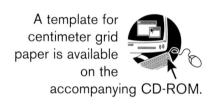

A template for centimeter grid paper is available on the accompanying CD-ROM.

Materials and Equipment

For each student—
- A copy of the activity sheet "Double-Dare Situation"
- A copy of the activity sheet "Double-Dare Simulation"
- A copy of the activity sheet "Double-Dare Theory"
- A copy of the activity sheet "Double-Dare with Algebra"
- One or two sheets of grid paper

For each pair of students—
- Two paper bags: a bag labeled "Bag 1," containing three blue cubes and one yellow cube; and a bag labeled "Bag 2," containing two red cubes and one yellow cube. The cubes should be the same size. (Note: Other objects, such as small balls or marbles, can work just as well as cubes for this activity; and the teacher can use a color other than yellow as the third color.)

For each group of four students (optional)—
- Blank transparencies and markers

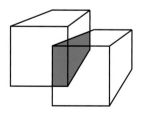

Discussion

Double-Dare is designed for a class that is unfamiliar with the concept of expected value or the use of simulations. It assumes that the students can set up and solve linear equations. The activity is appropriate in conjunction with the study of probability and can serve as an interesting application of linear equations.

In some games, such as backgammon, when player A is ahead, she or he can "double" the other player, player B. By doubling, player A asks player B either to quit and give player A a point for winning or to continue to play for a double score (two points). In such a situation, the question is whether player B stands to lose more points in the long run if she or he always gives up immediately (and loses one point) or if he or she always plays on, thereby sometimes winning two points and sometimes losing two points. The goal of this activity is to determine when it is better to use the "I-quit" strategy and when it is better to use the "play on" strategy.

To prepare for the activity, have pairs of students play a little game, "Don't Make Purple." In this game, player A draws a cube from bag 1 and a cube from bag 2. If the colors on the cubes "make purple"—that is, if one cube is blue and the other is red—then player A loses and his or her opponent, player B, receives a point. Opponents take turns drawing, and each player returns the cubes to their original bags after each play.

After students have played "Don't Make Purple" several times, introduce them to the "double-dare" option. Under this option, when player A draws a blue cube from bag 1, player B can double-dare him or her to continue. Player A now has a two-thirds chance of drawing a red cube from bag 2, thereby losing the game. If player A accepts the double and does lose, player B will earn two points. If player A refuses the double-dare challenge, player B receives one point and the game ends. After playing this variation of the game several times, students should understand how the double-dare concept works and be ready to begin the activity Double-Dare.

Part 1—"The Double-Dare Situation"

Start the Double-Dare activity by asking a student to read aloud "The Double-Dare Situation." This scenario asks students to imagine that they are playing a game and have fallen behind. In fact, they know that their probability of losing is two-thirds and their probability of winning is one-third. Their opponent doubles. The students must decide whether in such a situation they should always accept the challenge to play for double points or whether they should always quit and concede a point. Ask a number of students to explain the situation in their own words until you are confident that every student understands the problem.

Part 2—"Double-Dare Simulation"

When you are certain that the students understand doubling, you can set them to work on "Double-Dare Simulation." Conduct several simulations with the class, following the directions on the activity sheet, to ensure that the students grasp the process. Then ask the students to work with partners on the worksheet. When the pairs have finished the simulation in number 2 and have completed chart 1, have them enter their results in chart 2 (see fig. 4.5).

After all pairs of students have entered their results in the chart, discuss the results. Students will probably be disappointed because most of their total scores will be negative; however, in this game, losing as little as possible is important. The students need to realize that in the long run, the less negative the score, the better the strategy.

Most students will find that accepting the double and playing on is actually the best strategy. Remind them, however, that they have considered only the situation in which the probability of losing is two-thirds. Ask them whether they think that accepting the double is always better, in every situation. For instance, suppose that in "Don't Make Purple" a player draws first from bag 2, which contains two red cubes and a yellow cube, and then from bag 1, which contains three blue cubes and one yellow cube. If the player draws a red cube from bag 2, his or her probability of losing on the next draw is three-fourths.

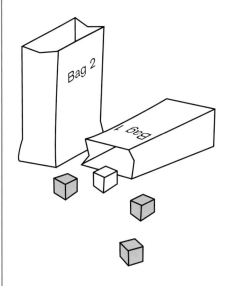

Strategy	Number of Games Won	Number of Games Lost	Number of Points Won	Number of Points Lost	Total Score
"Play on"					
"I quit"					

Fig. **4.5.**

A sample chart, like chart 2 on the activity sheet, for organizing the results of the simulations

Students can simulate this situation and determine the optimal strategy when the probability of losing is three-fourths. Would the player be wise to accept a double in this case? Explain that checking all the probabilities with simulations would be too time-consuming. The students will readily understand that if they are certain to lose, they do not want to accept a double. Therefore, they need to use the theory of probability to see what will happen in the long run for various situations. The next part of the activity, "Double-Dare Theory," takes the students through some of the basics.

Part 3—"Double-Dare Theory"

In contrast with "Double-Dare Simulation," which introduces the idea of expected value by using actual data from simulated games, "Double-Dare Theory" develops the idea by considering the probabilities of winning and losing in a large number of hypothetical games. Without doing a simulation or computation, students should realize that if they always use the "I quit" strategy, their expected value will be –1. The first question on the "Double-Dare Theory" activity sheet gives you a chance to assess whether they understand this idea.

To determine the expected value for the strategy of accepting the double, students imagine a large number of games and compute the number of games that they can expect to win or lose, given a particular probability of losing. They calculate the expected total of their scores for all the games and divide this score by the number of games to obtain the average score per game. This average is the theoretical expected value.

Textbooks compute expected values by multiplying the number of points won or lost by their respective probabilities and adding the results. In the case where players always accept the double challenge, this process yields the following expected value:

$$EV = \frac{2}{3}(-2 \text{ points}) + \frac{1}{3}(2 \text{ points}) = -\frac{2}{3} \text{ point}.$$

Even though this method of computing the expected value is efficient, it is not very enlightening in a student's first encounter with the concept. "Double-Dare Theory" therefore approaches the notion of expected value in a more concrete fashion by asking the students to consider what would happen if someone played a large number of games under the circumstances described in the activity.

In the final steps of "Double-Dare Theory," the students find the expected values for different probabilities of losing. After each pair of students has worked on three probabilities in addition to the two-thirds probability, they discuss with another pair of students the circumstances under which the "I quit" strategy is best. When all the groups have finished, ask them to post their results on the board or on an overhead transparency, and then conduct a whole-class discussion of the data. The students should see that if the probability of losing is below a certain "break-even point," the best strategy is to play on; however, if the probability is above that point, they should quit. When the probability of losing equals the break-even probability, the expected values for each strategy are equal.

Part 4—"Double-Dare with Algebra"

The "Double-Dare with Algebra" activity sheet guides students through an algebraic method for determining the break-even point. On the basis of their work in "Double-Dare Theory," the students might be able to guess that the break-even point is a three-fourths probability of losing. The use of algebra, however, enables students to confirm or reject their conjectures. The activity sheet "Double-Dare with Algebra" leads students to an equation that they can solve to find the break-even point. If they play 100 games with a probability P of losing, they can expect to lose $P(100)$ games and win $(1 - P)(100)$ games. If they use the strategy of playing on, the total points, won or lost, for the 100 games is $2(1 - P)(100) - 2P(100)$. If they use the strategy of rejecting the double, the point total for 100 games would be -100. Thus, the break-even point in the probabilities is the solution to the following equation:

$$2(1 - P)(100) - 2P(100) = -100.$$

After simplification, the result becomes $2(1 - P) - 2P = -1$, or $3 = 4P$. The break-even point is thus $P = .75$.

Assessment

To develop integrative habits of mind, you should be sure that your assessments focus on application, analysis, and synthesis. Teachers who focus only on lower-level understanding, such as the ability to solve an equation for the break-even point, will shortchange their students. There are many effective ways to use the "looking-back" strategies that Pólya (1973) suggests in his problem-solving model to assess students' understanding and help them appreciate the integrative power of these processes. The following assessment suggestions illustrate this point.

Several times in this activity, the students compute expected values by analyzing a large number of hypothetical games under the assumption that the probability of losing is two-thirds. Whether the number of games is 30 or 75, the expected value associated with a playing strategy is the same. For example, if the probability of losing is P and if someone uses the "play on" strategy in N games, then the expected value of the "play on" strategy is

$$\frac{2(1-P)N - 2PN}{N}.$$

Simplifying this expression results in an expected value for the strategy of $2(1 - P) - 2P$, regardless of N. This expression is the one that text-book methods yield for the expected value. However, without using the connective processes involved in the looking-back phase of problem solving, students probably would not recognize that the expected value is independent of the number of games.

To assess the depth of your students' understanding of expected value, as well as their ability to consolidate their results, challenge them to explore whether the expected value depends on the number of games in the averaging process in "Double-Dare Theory." You might ask the students to write a journal entry or to create a poster after they have completed the activity sheet for "Double-Dare Theory."

You can offer a similar challenge, which is indeed an extension of the preceding line of reasoning, after students have completed the activity sheet for "Double-Dare with Algebra." Ask them to explore, in a journal entry or poster presentation, whether the break-even point depends on the number of games. Students who truly understand that the

Georg Pólya's (1973) problem-solving model includes four phases of problem solving: "First, we have to *understand* the problem; we have to see clearly what is required. Second, we have to see how the various items are connected, how the unknown is linked to the data, in order to obtain the idea of the solution, to make a *plan*. Third, we *carry out* our plan. Fourth, we *look back* at the completed solution, we review and discuss it." (p. 5)

expected value is independent of the number of games can apply their insight to proving that the break-even point does not depend on the number of games. However, you should encourage students to revisit their simulation and discover that the chances of getting close to the expected value increase as the number of games increases.

Where to Go Next in Instruction

Double-Dare starts with a real-world problem, uses simulation to deepen students' understanding of the problem, and connects probabilistic reasoning with algebraic methods to solve the problem and extend the results. It illustrates how mathematical questions can become the integrative problems that *Principles and Standards* calls for by taking advantage of the full richness of the problem-solving process as described by Pólya.

Chapter 4's final activity, Support Cables, focuses on the looking-back process as a means for developing the integrative potential of a problem. By devising, connecting, simplifying, generalizing, and extending alternative solutions to a problem, students engage in the processes that ultimately lead to an integration of mathematics at the cognitive level.

Support Cables

Goals

Work with the support-cables problem to—
- Develop empirical solutions
- Develop generalized solutions
- Use technology to lend rigor to empirical solutions
- Demonstrate the need for proof of empirical solutions
- Apply properties of similar triangles and analytic geometry

Materials and Equipment

For each student—
- A copy of the activity sheet "Measuring the Middle Pole"
- A copy of the activity sheet "Interactive Measurement"
- A copy of the activity sheet "Proving Your Conjecture"
- A copy of the activity sheet "Is There a Better Way?"
- A ruler
- One or two sheets of grid paper

For each group of two or three students—
- Access to a computer and to the applet Support Cables (available on the CD-ROM) or access to interactive geometry software

pp. 151–52; 153; 154–55; 156

A template for centimeter grid paper is available on the accompanying CD-ROM.

Discussion

This activity presents a problem that students can readily solve by using similar triangles or analytic geometry:

To ensure the safety of its trapeze artists, a circus secures its trapezes with a structure of interconnected poles, cables, and nets. Figure 4.6 shows a small portion of one such structure. In this arrangement, support cables connect two poles—one 30 feet tall and the other 24 feet tall. A cable connects the top of each pole to the base of the opposite pole. A third pole secures the cables at the point where they intersect.

What is the height (h) of the middle pole? Does h depend on the distance between the outer poles?

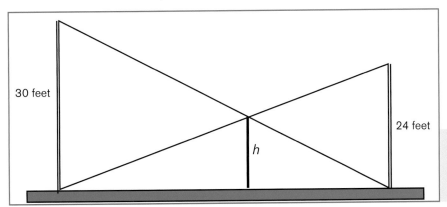

30 feet

24 feet

h

Fig. **4.6.**

A section of a network of poles and cables supporting circus trapezes

As Pólya (1973) notes in his classic *How to Solve It* (p. 5), once students have understood a problem and have formulated a plan for solving it, their next interaction with the problem should be carrying out the plan and obtaining a solution. The first part of the activity encourages students to use an empirical method (measuring) to solve the problem. Students subsequently use interactive geometry software to test their solutions, and in the process they examine the generality of the solutions. The need to establish the truth of their generalizations leads naturally to proof and a variety of problem-solving approaches. Thus, by considering alternative strategies, looking back at their initial solutions, and seeking to improve and extend their results, the students learn to consolidate their knowledge and connect mathematical content and representations.

The problem of the poles and cables is subtle in its complexity and capable of eliciting rich mathematical explorations. Students typically recognize the similar triangles in the figure, but the lack of information tends to trouble them. If the distance between the poles is unknown, how can they solve the problem? The solution involves the discovery that the distance between the two outer poles is irrelevant. The irrelevance of the distance, however, is not readily apparent. Moreover, students often have difficulty representing the variable (or unknown) components of the problem, much less working with these variables. Thus, initial empirical explorations of the problem can be very beneficial.

Part 1—"Measuring the Middle Pole"

The most direct path to a solution is to measure the height of the middle pole. Students can use grid paper to draw the two outer poles to scale, sketch the supporting wires and middle pole, and measure the height of the middle pole. Of course, such length measurements will not be exact. The students should recognize this limitation of their results and use them with caution. Nonetheless, this empirical approach allows students to investigate whether the distance between the outer poles affects the solution. The task in number 3 on the activity sheet helps the students develop a compelling case for their conjectures. You should assign each student a different distance to use for the task.

For example, each unit on the grid in figure 4.7 represents 2 feet. In the sketch on the left, the outer poles are 40 feet apart, as in number 2 on the activity sheet. However, in the sketch on the right, they are a different number of feet apart, as in number 3. Here they are 30 feet apart.

Nevertheless, in both situations, the support cables appear to meet at a height that is close to the true value of h—$13\frac{1}{3}$ feet. In fact, all students should find that the height of the middle pole is between 12

If the distance between the poles is unknown, how can students solve the problem?

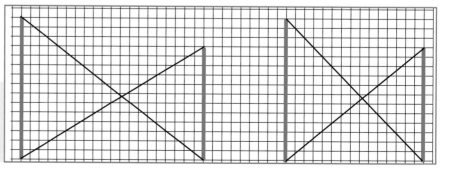

Fig. **4.7.**

Empirical evidence that the height of the middle pole is constant regardless of the distance between the outer poles

and 14 feet. Although this result does not prove the irrelevance of the distance between the outer poles, these empirical investigations certainly suggest that the height of the middle pole is not dependent on this distance.

Part 2—"Interactive Measurement"

As a follow-up to hands-on measurement, students can explore the problem by using interactive geometry software or the applet Support Cables on the CD-ROM accompanying this book. The applet allows students to manipulate the distance between the poles and observe the height of the middle pole. This dynamic representation gives students a more precise and compelling demonstration of the fact that the height remains constant. If the students are using interactive geometry software, they should follow the instructions on the activity sheet "Interactive Measurement."

Students can also use interactive geometry software such as The Geometer's Sketchpad to model the problem.

Part 3—"Proving Your Conjecture"

On the basis of parts 1 and 2, the students should conjecture that the height of the middle pole does not depend on the distance between the two end poles. In this third exploration, they use deductive strategies to prove that this conjecture is true and to determine the height of the middle pole. The first strategy in this exploration is geometric and uses the similar triangles and parallel lines in the problem's diagram. Figure 4.8 shows the diagram that the students work with to identify all the pairs of similar triangles. Students should provide some justification when they claim that two triangles are similar.

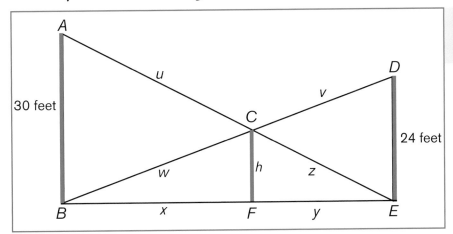

Fig. **4.8.**

Support cables with the unknowns labeled

By using the fact that $\triangle ABC \sim \triangle EDC$, the students can generate the equations

$$\frac{w}{v} = \frac{u}{z} = \frac{30}{24}.$$

Because $\overline{CF} \parallel \overline{AB}$, the students can apply the parallel projection theorem to find that

$$\frac{u}{z} = \frac{x}{y}.$$

Thus, by substitution,

$$\frac{30}{24} = \frac{x}{y}.$$

The parallel projection theorem states that for any triangle ABC with $D \in$ interior $\overline{AB}$ and $E \in$ interior $\overline{AC}$, $\overline{DE} \parallel \overline{BC}$ if and only if

$$\frac{DB}{DA} = \frac{EC}{EA}.$$

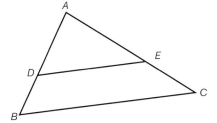

Simplifying and solving for x give

$$x = \frac{5y}{4}.$$

By using the fact that $\triangle ABE \sim \triangle CFE$, the students can obtain

$$\frac{h}{30} = \frac{y}{x+y}.$$

Substituting $x = \frac{5y}{4}$ yields the result

$$\frac{h}{30} = \frac{y}{\frac{5y}{4} + y} = \frac{y}{2.25y} = \frac{1}{2.25}.$$

Thus,

$$h = \frac{30}{2.25} = 13\frac{1}{3} \text{ feet.}$$

When students look back at their work, they should note that although the calculations involve x and y, they do not affect the final answer. The height is independent of the distance $x + y$.

The second strategy for solving the problem uses analytic geometry. The students construct a diagram of the structure of poles and cables in the xy-coordinate plane, as in figure 4.9, and they label each of the "corner" points.

Fig. **4.9.**

To approach the problem with analytic geometry, the students superimpose a diagram of the structure of poles and cables on a coordinate grid

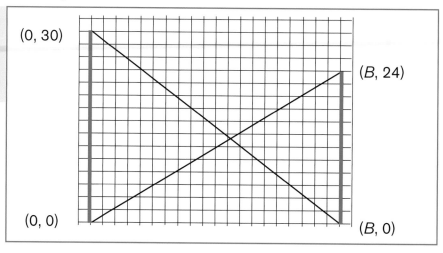

They then must find equations for the line containing points $(0, 0)$ and $(B, 24)$ and the line containing points $(0, 30)$ and $(B, 0)$. The slope of the line joining the points $(0, 0)$ and $(B, 24)$ is $24/B$, so the equation of the line containing these points is

$$y = \frac{24}{B}x, \text{ or } x = \frac{B \cdot y}{24}.$$

Likewise, the line containing the points $(0, 30)$ and $(B, 0)$ has slope $-30/B$ and y-intercept 30, so the equation of this line is

$$y = 30 - \frac{30}{B}x.$$

Next, the students must find the point of intersection of the two lines. To obtain the y-coordinate of the point, they can eliminate x in

$$y = 30 - \frac{30}{B}x,$$

by substituting for x:

$$x = \frac{B \cdot y}{24}.$$

Thus,

$$y = 30 - \frac{30}{B}\left(\frac{B \cdot y}{24}\right),$$

or, after simplifying,

$$y = 13\frac{1}{3}.$$

Like the previous strategy, this strategy proves that the solution does not depend on B, the distance between the poles.

Part 4—"Is There a Better Way?"

In part 3, the strategies with similar triangles and analytic geometry both use algebraic and proportional reasoning with multiple variables. Such reasoning is often difficult for students, who may need some guidance through the steps. However, when they look back on their solutions, you should challenge them to consider whether they can find an easier way to arrive at the result. After all, since the solution involved finding a value for only one of the variables, h, perhaps there is an argument that uses only h. Part 4 provides students with a hint and points them to a shorter solution. It then asks them to generalize their results by considering how high the middle pole would be when the heights of the outer poles are p and q, respectively.

Figure 4.10 shows the diagram that the students consider in part 4. The auxiliary segment $\overline{RS}$ contains C and is perpendicular to the outer poles. The corresponding altitudes in the similar triangles ABC and EDC are $\overline{RC}$ and $\overline{SC}$, and they divide the sides $\overline{AB}$ and $\overline{ED}$ into corresponding segments. Because $\overline{RB}$ corresponds to $\overline{SD}$,

$$\frac{RB}{SD} = \frac{30}{24}.$$

Thus, since $RB = h$ and $SD = 24 - h$, the students get the equation

$$\frac{h}{24 - h} = \frac{30}{24}.$$

They can easily solve this equation and generalize it for outer poles of length p and q:

$$\frac{h}{q - h} = \frac{p}{q},$$

which yields

$$h = \frac{pq}{p + q}.$$

Assessment

Parts 3 and 4 of Support Cables assume that students are familiar with setting up proportions that are based on similar triangles and segments cut by parallel lines, as well as with setting up and solving

Fig. **4.10.**

$\overline{RB}$ corresponds to $\overline{SD}$, and $\overline{AB}$ corresponds to $\overline{ED}$

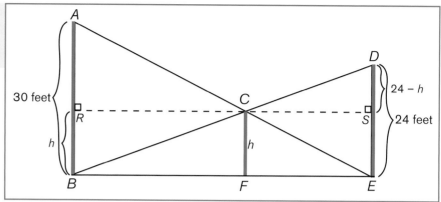

systems of linear equations. Before assigning students these explorations, you should assess their readiness. You can use the explorations to review these concepts.

For some students, the single-variable approach in part 4 may be more accessible than the multiple-variable approach of part 3. However, the single-variable approach depends on the insight that in similar triangles, corresponding segments—not just sides—are in the same proportion. A discussion of this idea should compare the proportions of corresponding altitudes, medians, and other segments of two similar triangles. The use of interactive geometry software to measure and find the ratios of corresponding segments can facilitate this discussion.

You can also use the unifying idea of transformations to argue the case. Any two similar triangles with correspondence ratio k are congruent to similar triangles related by a dilation $D(x, y) = (kx, ky)$, as illustrated in figure 4.11. Therefore, if (x_1, y_1) and (x_2, y_2) are two points on $\triangle OAB$, then the corresponding points on $\triangle OA'B'$ are (kx_1, ky_1) and (kx_2, ky_2). The distance between the two points on $\triangle OAB$ is

$$\sqrt{(x_2 - x_1)^2 + (y_2 - y_1)^2}.$$

The distance between their corresponding points on $\triangle OA'B'$ is

$$\sqrt{(kx_2 - kx_1)^2 + (ky_2 - ky_1)^2},$$

which simplifies to

$$k\sqrt{(x_2 - x_1)^2 + (y_2 - y_1)^2}.$$

Thus, the ratio of all segments corresponding under the dilation mapping is k.

Fig. **4.11.**

$\triangle UVT \cong \triangle OAB$, $\triangle RST \cong \triangle OA'B'$,
$D(\triangle OAB) = \triangle OA'B'$

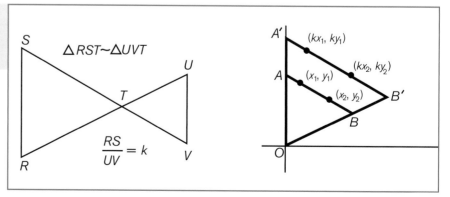

Students can associate many connective processes in the looking-back phase of problem solving. In fact, Pólya claimed that the looking-back phase is limitless because "no problem whatever is completely exhausted" (Pólya 1973, p. 15). Specialization is one of the connective processes that Pólya suggests. To learn whether your students are able to make their own connections, challenge them to solve the support-cable problem for the situation in which the outer poles are the same height. In this special case, the ends of the outer poles form a rectangle, with the cables as the diagonals. Students can readily solve the problem by considering the properties of rectangles, and the invariance of the answer may be easier for them to see.

Pólya suggests another connective strategy that you can use in assessing your students' understanding. Pose Pólya's question, "Can you use the result, or the method, for some other problem?" (Pólya 1973, p. 16). For example, if students know the height of the middle pole and the height of one of the outer poles, can they find the height of the other outer pole? Under what conditions is determining a height for the other pole impossible? Students can work with their generalized solution,

$$h = \frac{pq}{p+q},$$

and use algebra to show that

$$p = \frac{qh}{q-h}$$

and that the problem has a solution only when the height of the middle pole is less than the height of the outer poles.

Conclusion

A thorough exploration of Support Cables draws on numerous mathematical content areas and processes. It meshes empirical and deductive strategies, as well as geometric and algebraic approaches. It uses technology to provide dynamic representations and by-hand methods to facilitate the formulation of a conjecture. Like other activities in this volume, it emphasizes proportional reasoning, one of the key unifying processes in high school mathematics. Students can find the solution to the problem in one of several ways; but by emphasizing the integrative processes of alternative methods and having the students look back, you can lead them to a richer understanding of the problem.

"One of the first and foremost duties of the teacher is not to give his [or her] students the impression that mathematical problems have little connection with each other, and no connection at all with anything else. We have a natural opportunity to investigate the connections of a problem when looking back at its solution." (Pólya 1973, p. 15)

NAVIGATING *through* MATHEMATICAL CONNECTIONS

Looking Back and Looking Ahead

The mathematical habit of mind looks for connections, common patterns, and logical coherence in mathematical phenomena. This habit has led to a mathematics discipline that is highly integrated within itself and with other disciplines. The modeling and problem-solving processes that this book has emphasized are intrinsic to the mathematical habit of mind and figure prominently in NCTM's *Principles and Standards for School Mathematics* (NCTM 2000) as goals for our mathematics curriculum. Who could take issue with the vision of student learning set forth in *Principles and Standards*?

> Students confidently engage in complex mathematical tasks chosen carefully by teachers. They draw on knowledge from a wide variety of mathematical topics, sometimes approaching the same problem from different mathematical perspectives or representing the mathematics in different ways until they find methods that enable them to make progress. Teachers help students make, refine, and explore conjectures on the basis of evidence and use a variety of reasoning and proof techniques to confirm or disprove those conjectures. Students are flexible and resourceful problem solvers. Alone or in groups and with access to technology, they work productively and reflectively, with the skilled guidance of their teachers. Orally and in writing, students communicate their ideas and results effectively. They value mathematics and engage actively in learning it. (NCTM 2000, p. 3)

We have tried to capture this vision in sample activities that illustrate the integrative potential of modeling and problem-solving processes as well as unifying mathematical concepts. However, the vision in *Principles and Standards* presents a challenge that goes beyond any such set of activities. Activities similar to those in this volume, no matter how rich and motivating they are, do not by themselves constitute a coherent, connected curriculum. In fact, unrelated "rich" activities, taught separately and without a common core focus or unifying theme, have little hope of achieving NCTM's vision of curricular coherence or of helping students achieve deep and lasting mathematical understandings.

If teachers and curriculum designers truly wish to integrate the mathematical experiences of students, they must work together to weave strong conceptual connections between day-to-day and year-to-year learning experiences. Doing so demands concerted efforts to connect the content strands of the Standards with core, unifying ideas and to embed the integrative modeling and problem-solving processes into the normal routine of the mathematics curriculum. With *Principles and Standards for School Mathematics* (NCTM 2000), the National Council of Teachers of Mathematics has gone on record as affirming that the mathematical experience of our students can be integrated and that achieving the vision of coherent, connected learning is within our reach.

NAVIGATIONS
SERIES

GRADES 9–12

NAVIGATING
through
MATHEMATICAL
CONNECTIONS

Appendix
Blackline Masters and Solutions

Breath by Breath

Name _____

Growing Balloons—Part 1

Your teacher has given your group a balloon. Select one member of the group to inflate the balloon, one breath at a time, and a second group member to measure the circumference of a great circle of the balloon, in centimeters, after each breath. The third member of your group will record the data as the balloon grows larger.

Each breath should contain about the same volume of air. In addition, a breath should not be so large that the balloon reaches its capacity in just two or three breaths. To develop a uniform technique, practice inflating the balloon before gathering your data.

1. When you are ready to begin, inflate the balloon, breath by breath. Measure its circumference after each breath, and enter your data in the chart. (Group members who are inflating and measuring can copy the recorder's data onto their own activity sheets when they have finished working with the balloon.)

Number of Breaths	Circumference (cm)

2. *a.* Enter your group's data into a graphing calculator, and graph the balloon's circumference against the number of breaths that you used to inflate it.

Navigating through Mathematical Connections in Grades 9–12

Breath by Breath (continued)

Name _____

b. Sketch the graph of the data in the space below, making sure to calibrate your graph.

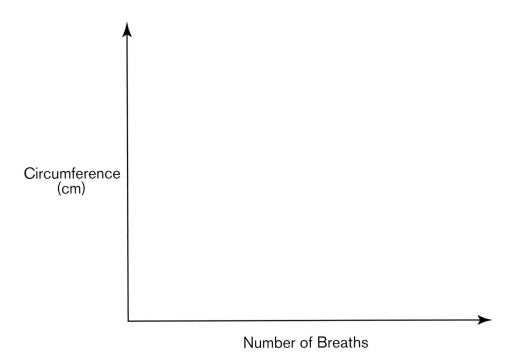

3. *a.* Find a function that fits your data well, and write it here.

b. Explain how effective you think your function is as a model of your data.

c. Show a sketch of a graph of your function on the same axes that you used to sketch your graph in number 2.

Take a Breath and Theorize

Name _____

Growing Balloons—Part 2

Scientific theories are conjectures about relationships among experimental variables. In part 2 of the activity Growing Balloons, you will extend your work with your balloon from part 1 to develop a formula that gives the circumference (c) of the balloon *in theory*, in terms of the number (b) of breaths that someone might blow into it.

In part 1, you tried to make each breath of air that went into the balloon the same size. Thus, you can say theoretically that each breath contributes the same volume of air to the balloon. You can think of each breath as a unit of volume that is equivalent to a number (k) of cubic centimeters (cm^3). Therefore, $\sqrt[3]{k}$ is equivalent to a length in centimeters (cm).

In addition, at any given stage ($b = 1$, $b = 2$, $b = 3$, etc.) in your balloon's growth, the number of breaths times the volume of each breath, $b \times k$, is also a volume that is equivalent to a number of cubic centimeters. Thus, $\sqrt[3]{bk}$ is also equivalent to a length in centimeters.

Remember that in part 1 you worked with the balloon's circumference (c) as a measure of length in centimeters. Consequently, you might speculate that the value of c, which changes as the value of b changes, is related in some way to $\sqrt[3]{bk}$, or $\sqrt[3]{b} \times \sqrt[3]{k}$, since they have the same units—centimeters. But $\sqrt[3]{k}$ is a constant, so a good assumption to investigate is the idea that c is proportional to $\sqrt[3]{b}$.

1. Assume that your balloon is spherical. Write a formula for the circumference of a great circle of the balloon in terms of its radius (r).

   $c =$ _____

   Also write a formula for the volume (v) of the balloon in terms of its radius (r).

   $v =$ _____

2. Using your formula for the balloon's volume (v), solve for r in terms of v.

   $r =$ _____

3. Using your formula for r, express the circumference of your balloon in terms of its volume.

   $c =$ _____

4. You are assuming that each breath adds the same volume of air (k cm^3) to the balloon. What is the relationship between the number of breaths (b) and the volume of the balloon (v)?

   $v =$ _____

5. Combine your answers to numbers 3 and 4 to find a relationship between the circumference of the balloon and the number of breaths.

   $c =$ _____

Take a Breath and Theorize (continued)

Name _____

6. By factoring the expression on the right side of the equation in number 5, complete the following formula:

    $c =$ _____ $\cdot \sqrt[3]{b}$

7. The equation in number 6 has the form $c = m \cdot \sqrt[3]{b}$, where m is a constant. This form indicates that c is directly proportional to $\sqrt[3]{b}$. It also indicates that m is the slope of the line $y = mx$, where y stands for the circumference of the balloon, and x stands for the cube root of the number of breaths of air that someone blows into it. Use your balloon data from part 1 to complete the following chart:

Number (b) of Breaths	$\sqrt[3]{b}$	Circumference (c) (cm)

Draw a scatterplot on the axes shown, relating the second and third columns of your chart:

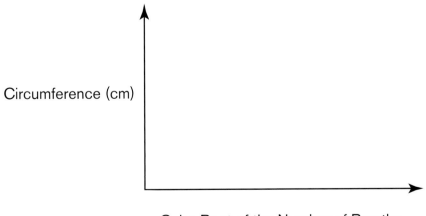

Name _____

8. Find the slope (m) of a line through the origin that is a good fit for the data in your scatterplot. Use this value to simplify the formula that you gave in number 6.

   $c =$ _____ $\cdot \sqrt[3]{b}$

9. Compare your theoretical formula in number 8 with the function that you found in part 1, in 3(a). Does your theoretical result in part 2 support your earlier empirical result? _____ Explain.

Experimenting with a Dosage

Name _____

Healthy Dose—Part 1

Suppose that a drug company has established that a patient must have 40 milligrams of a certain prescription drug in the body for the drug to be effective. Moreover, the company's studies indicate that anything in excess of 600 milligrams is toxic, and its research has shown that the body eliminates 10 percent of the drug every four hours.

Imagine that you are a doctor prescribing this drug for a patient. How often would you want your patient to take the drug, and in what quantity, to ensure effectiveness while avoiding toxicity?

Assume that the drug is absorbed quickly and completely into the patient's body. (This is true of intravenous drugs; in actual practice, a fraction of an oral dose breaks down in the stomach and is eliminated before entering the bloodstream.)

1. Select a dose of the drug for your patient to take at 0 hours.

   a. Enter this dose in the chart, in the row for time 0 and the column labeled "Amount of Drug in the Body (mg)."

Time (hr)	Amount of Drug in the Body (mg)
0	
4	
8	
12	
16	
20	
24	

   b. How did you select your initial dose?

2. a. Complete the chart in number 1 to show the amount of the drug remaining in the body at 4-hour intervals after the initial dose, over a 24-hour period.

   b. How did you determine the amount of the drug remaining in the body at the end of each 4-hour interval?

3. a. Was your initial dose effective over an entire 24-hour period?_____ If not, for how long was it effective? _____

Experimenting with a Dosage (continued)

Name _____

b. What are the advantages to having a dosage that remains effective over a 24-hour period?

c. If your initial dose was not effective for 24 hours, select a new dose that you think will be, and complete a new chart.

Time (hr)	Amount of Drug in the Body (mg)
0	
4	
8	
12	
16	
20	
24	

d. Adjust your dose if necessary to obtain a dose that is effective over an entire 24-hour period.

4. a. What percentage of your initial dose remains in the body after 24 hours? _____

   b. What percentage did the body eliminate in that time? _____

5. a. Determine a function that describes the amount of drug in the body at any time t after the initial dose.

   b. Explain how you developed your function.

Fine-Tuning a Dosage and a Schedule

Name _____

Healthy Dose—Part 2

Again consider the drug that you examined in part 1 of Healthy Dose. For the drug to be effective, a patient must have 40 milligrams of the drug in his or her system. To avoid toxicity, the patient must have less than 600 milligrams of the drug in his or her body at all times. The patient's body eliminates 10 percent of the drug every 4 hours.

Suppose that you are a doctor, and you want to establish a dosage and a schedule that will be convenient, effective, and safe for your patient. (Again assume that the drug is absorbed quickly and completely into the patient's body.)

1. Assuming that 4 hours is the minimum time that patients must allow between doses, select a dose for your patient and a schedule for him or her to follow in taking the drug.

   a. Complete the chart to show the situation over the first 48 hours in which your patient takes the drug. Assume that the patient takes the first dose at 0 hours.

Time (hr)	Drug Dose (mg)	Amount of Drug in the Body (mg)
0		
4		
8		
12		
16		
20		
24		
28		
32		
36		
40		
44		
48		

   b. Does the dosage that you chose remain safe and effective over a period of 48 hours? _____

Name _____

c. If necessary, adjust the size of the dose or the patient's schedule for taking it to ensure that the drug is effective and safe at the end of 48 hours.

2. Use spreadsheet software or a similar tool to extend your chart to cover a one-week period, showing the patient's dosage, his or her schedule for taking new doses, and the amount of the drug remaining in his or her system at the end of each 4-hour interval.

   a. Does the drug remain effective and safe over the entire week? _____

   b. If necessary, adjust the dosage or the timetable to make the drug safe and effective over an entire week.

3. Suppose that you want your patient to continue to take the drug indefinitely. Justify your answers to the following questions with tables or graphs.

   a. Does the drug remain effective?

   b. Does it remain safe?

Scoping Out the Territory

Name _____

Nearest Neighbors—Part 1

Consider the following situations, each of which presents one or more problems for you to solve. Design a hypothetical case for each situation and develop a solution for each problem.

1. A large community has multiple elementary schools. The community leaders must decide which children should attend which schools. What criteria should they use in determining their policy?

2. Have you ever seen robins, squirrels, or other animals chasing each other away from a particular area? Many animals are territorial and will defend a space that they consider to be their own or that they use when they forage for food.

   a. What determines the territories that animals will defend?

   b. Are there patterns in how the territorial boundaries look?

3. A chain of identical pizzerias has a monopoly on the pizza business in a certain city.

   a. How do citizens decide which pizzeria to go to for pizza?

   b. Suppose that someone in the city wants to open a new pizzeria in the chain. What should he or she consider in deciding where to locate?

   c. Suppose that a competing chain wants to open some new pizzerias in the same city. What are the owners of this chain likely to consider in deciding where to build?

Name _____

4. The situations in numbers 1–3 have features in common that enable them to be modeled, or represented, in the same way mathematically.

   a. What are these similar features?

   b. Did your solutions make use of any common, underlying principles?

   c. Compare and discuss your responses with your classmates.

5. Draw a diagram that can model all the situations. *Hint:* Begin by placing four or five dots randomly in the box. Let the dots represent nests, schools, or pizzerias, and then draw boundary lines to determine the regions belonging to each dot.

Name _____

6. Compare your diagram with those of your classmates, and discuss any differences that you notice.

  a. How did you determine where to place the boundary lines?

  b. What is true about the points on these lines?

  c. What is true about the regions that these lines create?

Your diagram belongs to a class of representations called *Voronoi diagrams,* named for Georgy Voronoi (1868–1908), the mathematician who first studied the shapes in them.

Voronoi Vantage Points

Name _____

Nearest Neighbors—Part 2

Construct a Voronoi diagram of some aspect of the world around you. This open-ended activity will give you a chance to apply Voronoi diagrams, explore their relevance in a new setting, and perhaps gain insight into the setting. Possible projects include, but are not limited to, the following:

- An analysis of actual school districts. Compare ideal Voronoi districts with actual districts in your city and assess the discrepancies.

- An analysis of the actual locations of restaurants in a fast-food chain. Consider where you would open a restaurant in the same chain or in a competing one.

- Other demographic analyses. You might consider people's proximity to—
  - professional sports arenas;
  - the twenty-five largest cities in the United States;
  - major watersheds;
  - toxic waste sites;
  - fire stations.

- Chemical and geological modeling. Consider crystal growth, chemical reactions, the formation of cracks in mud or lava flows, etc.

- An analysis of measurements of rainfall over a large area. Instead of simply averaging data on rainfall, use a weighted average, with the weights proportional to the areas of the Voronoi regions surrounding each rainfall gauge.

- An analysis of measurements of a lake's volume. Your analysis would be similar to an analysis of rainfall measurements, but discrete readings of depth would replace readings from rain gauges.

Write a report on your project, making sure that you include the following:

1. A complete description of the context and the problem

2. A clear statement of the assumptions that you made in applying a Voronoi model

3. A clearly labeled diagram with a brief description of how you constructed it

4. A summary of the evidence that the model is useful in describing patterns in the context

5. A list of the questions of interest—especially mathematical ones—that have emerged in the modeling process

6. A list of real-world constraints that could limit the applicability of the model in specific real-world settings

Transformers

Name _____

The graph below shows a pole with a flag on it as a geometric figure in the Cartesian plane. The list of points *P* shown to the right determines the graph. The figure is produced by an *x-y* line plot that connects the points in the order in which they appear in the list.

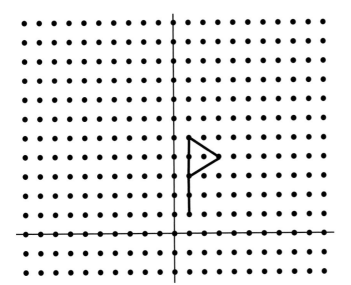

P	
x	*y*
1	1
1	5
3	4
1	3

Flag coordinates

1. Enter the coordinates of *P* into lists **L1** and **L2** on your calculator, and create a graph of the flag and flagpole. Use a window in which the squares appear to be square. (On the TI-83 Plus, try the window $-9 \leq x \leq 9$ and $-2 \leq y \leq 10$, with the format set to **GridOn**.)

2. To slide the flag's graph four units right and three units up, simply add 4 to the *x*-coordinates of *P* and add 3 to the *y*-coordinates. This transformation is called a *translation.* The new list of coordinates, denoted *P′*, is the "image" of *P*, and the rule for mapping the points of *P* to those of *P′* is denoted $T(x, y) = (x + 4, y + 3)$.

   a. Complete the list of values for *P′*.

   b. Plot the image in the grid at the right.

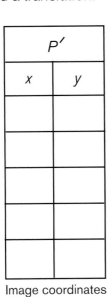

P′	
x	*y*

Image coordinates

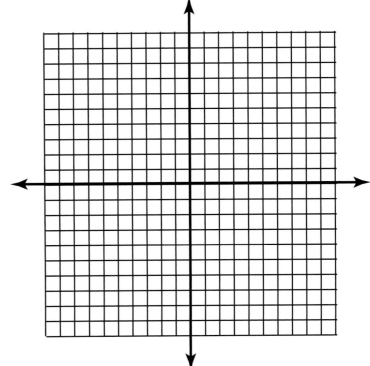

Transformers (continued)

Name _____

3. Produce the graph determined by *P'* on your calculator. Use **L3** for its *x*-coordinates and **L4** for its *y*-coordinates. You should obtain the picture at the right. *Hint:* Let **L3** = **L1** + 4, let **L4** = **L2** + 3, and turn on a new stat plot.

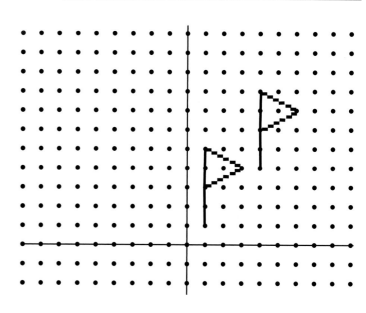

4. Use the transformation $r_{y\text{-axis}}(x, y) = (-x, y)$ to reflect *P* about the *y*-axis.

   a. Use this transformation to complete the list of values for the image of *P*.

   b. Graph the figure determined by *P'* in the grid at the right, as well as on a calculator.

P'	
x	y

Image coordinates

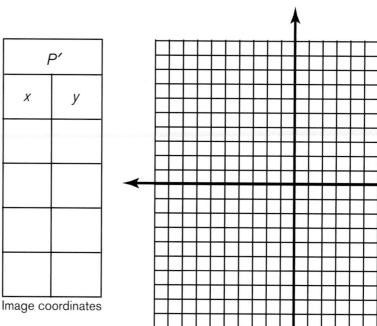

5. A *dilation* stretches or shrinks the figure determined by *P* without changing its proportions or the slope of its line segments. For example, the dilation $D(x, y) = (2x, 2y)$ transforms *P* so that *P'* yields a figure whose sides are double the length of the figure determined by *P*.

   a. Use this transformation to complete the list on the next page for *P'*.

   b. Plot the image in the grid on the next page, and plot the graph of *P'* on your calculator.

Navigating through Mathematical Connections in Grades 9–12

Transformers (continued)

Name _____

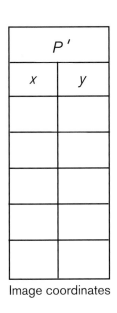

P'	
x	y

Image coordinates

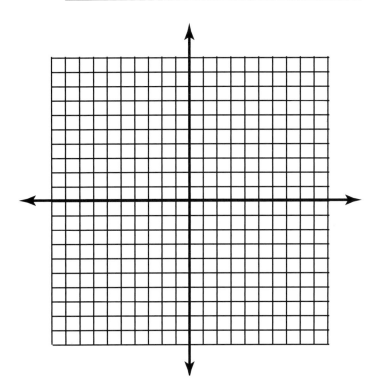

6. A transformation that stretches or shrinks *P* by different factors in the vertical and horizontal directions is called a *two-dimensional scale change.* For example, to transform *P* so that *P'* yields a figure with half the width and twice the height of the figure determined by *P,* use the scale change $S(x, y) =$ $(0.5x, 2y)$.

a. Use this transformation to complete the list of values for *P'*.

b. Plot the image in the grid to the right and on your calculator.

P'	
x	y

Image coordinates

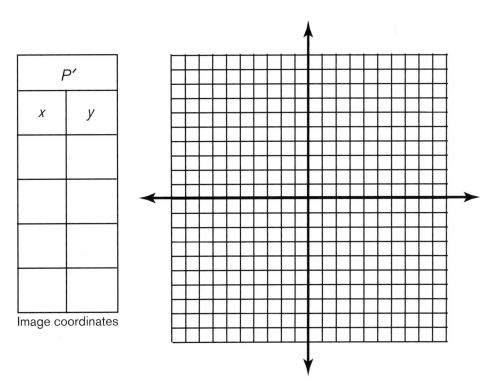

Transformers (continued)

7. *a.* Find the areas of the flags determined by *P* and by *P'* in step 5. Describe how the ratio of these two areas is related to the dilation $D(x, y) = (2x, 2y)$.

   b. Find the areas of the flags determined by *P* and by *P'* in step 6. Describe how the ratio of these areas is related to the scale change $S(x, y) = (0.5x, 2y)$.

8. Find a transformation rule for each of the following.

   a. Translate *P* so that the base of the flagpole is at $(-4, -1)$.

   b. Dilate *P* so that the area of the flag determined by *P'* is nine times that of *P*.

   c. Reflect *P* about the *x*-axis.

   d. Transform *P* so that the height of the flagpole determined by *P'* equals the horizontal width of its flag.

   e. Transform *P* so that *P'* is upside down, with the base of its flagpole located at $(-4, 6)$.

9. For the transformations defined in the previous steps, compare *P* with its image *P'*, and list the properties of *P* that changed after the transformation and those that remained the same. Your comparison of *P* with *P'* should consider such properties as location, distances, angle measures, proportions, areas, and orientation. (To determine whether the orientation has changed, choose three noncollinear points in the original figure, and check whether their positions relative to one another change in the image as you move clockwise from point to point.)

	Properties of the figure that change	Properties of the figure that remain the same
Translation		
Reflection		
Dilation		
Two-dimensional scale change		

The Function of Parents

Name _____

You can apply translations, reflections, and scale changes to the graphs of parent functions to generate other functions.

1. Suppose the line L is given by the equation $3x + 4y = 12$. Translate the line L five units to the left and two units up to produce the resulting image L'.

   a. Complete the list of selected values for L, and apply the translation rule to these points to fill in the list for L'.

   b. Plot graphs for L and L'.

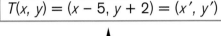

| L: 3x + 4y = 12 |

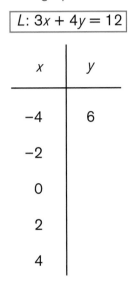

x	y
−4	6
−2	
0	
2	
4	

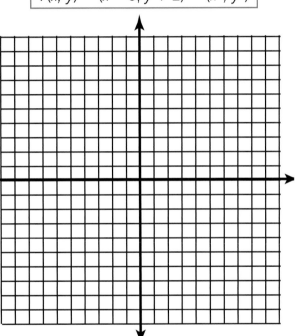

| L': |

x'	y'
−9	8
−7	

2. Use two points from the list to find the equation of the line L', and write it in the box above.

3. The x- and y-coordinates of line L satisfy the relation $3x + 4y = 12$. Also, since $x' = x - 5$ and $y' = y + 2$, the coordinates of points on L are related to the coordinates of their corresponding points on L' in the following ways: $x = x' + 5$ and $y = y' - 2$. By substituting these expressions for x and y into $3x + 4y = 12$, you can find a relation between the coordinates of the points on line L'. Find this relationship, and check whether the coordinates of L' in the list above fit the relationship.

4. a. Compare the equations for L' that you found in numbers 2 and 3. Are they equivalent?

The Function of Parents (continued)

Name _____

b. The inverse of $T(x, y) = (x - 5, y + 2)$ is a transformation that maps L' back to its preimage, L. The rule for this inverse is $T^{-1}(x, y) = (x + 5, y - 2)$. Check the points in the list for L' to see that $T^{-1}(x, y)$ in fact translates these points back to the points in L. Use number 3 as a guide to explain how the rule for $T^{-1}(x, y)$ can be computed from the rule for $T(x, y)$.

c. Use number 3 as a guide to explain how the equation of L and the expressions in $T^{-1}(x, y)$ can be used to find the equation for L'.

5. The following "connection diagram" summarizes the translation of line L to line L'. Note how the diagram uses the expressions from $T^{-1}(x, y)$ to generate the equation for L' from the equation for L.

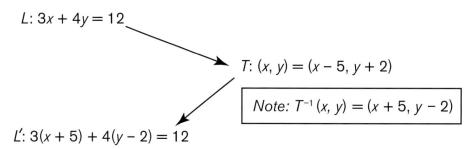

$L: 3x + 4y = 12$

$T: (x, y) = (x - 5, y + 2)$

Note: $T^{-1}(x, y) = (x + 5, y - 2)$

$L': 3(x + 5) + 4(y - 2) = 12$

a. Translate the graph of $P: y = x^2$ two units to the left and four units up, and draw the graph of P and the graph of its image P'.

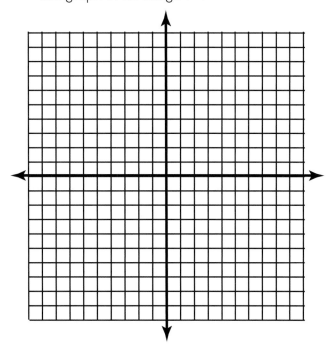

b. Complete the connection diagram and the note to show how to transform P to produce P'.

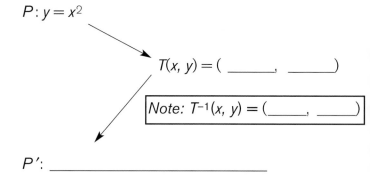

$P: y = x^2$

$T(x, y) = ($ _____ , _____ $)$

Note: $T^{-1}(x, y) = ($ _____ , _____ $)$

$P':$ _____

The Function of Parents (continued)

Name _____

6. The function $y = x^2$ and another quadratic function are graphed below. By using a scale change, you can keep the vertices fixed at (0, 0) and transform $y = x^2$ to generate the other quadratic.

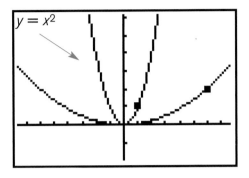

a. The scale change $S(x, y) = (6x, 2y)$ maps the point (1, 1) on the $y = x^2$ graph to the point (6, 2) on the other quadratic. Create a connection diagram for this transformation, and use a graphing calculator to check your results.

b. Find a scale change that maps the point (2, 4) on the graph of $y = x^2$ to the point (6, 2) on the other quadratic. Create a connection diagram for this transformation, and compare the function rule that you obtain with the function rule that you obtained in number 6(a).

c. To transform the graph of quadratic function P to the graph of quadratic function P', you can simply map the vertex of P and one other point on P to the vertex of P' and one other point on P', respectively. Use your answers in 6(a) and (b) to explain how you can do this in many ways.

d. Is the image of a parabola under a scale change always a parabola? Justify your answer.

Name _____

7. Starting from $y = x^2$, explain how to obtain the parabola graphed at the bottom of the following connection diagram. Its vertex is at $(-6, 7)$, and it passes through the point $(5, -1)$. Start with $y = x^2$, and complete the entire connection diagram. Use your calculator to check your answer as you go along.

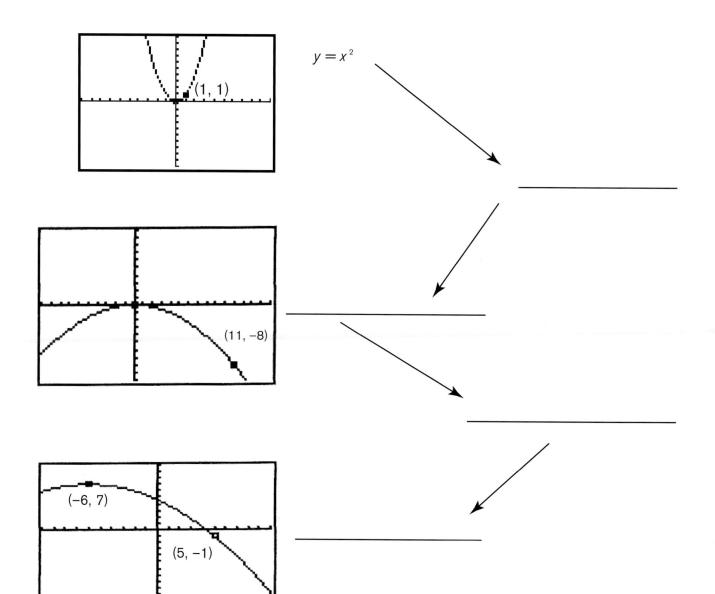

Slinky Transformations

Name _____

Periodic functions repeat themselves at regular intervals. Many real-world phenomena exhibit behavior that can be modeled with periodic functions. In this activity, you will use a periodic function to model the motion of a spring.

The data in the chart below were obtained by someone holding a Slinky spring toy above a motion sensor and allowing it to oscillate:

x (sec)	1.247	1.419	1.505	1.591	1.677	1.849	2.021	2.150	2.236	2.322	2.451	
y (m)	0.414	0.198	0.159	0.120	0.150	0.402	0.648	0.774	0.793	0.768	0.568	

x (sec)	2.623	2.752	2.838	2.924	3.096	3.268	3.354	3.440	3.526	3.612	3.698	3.870
y (m)	0.320	0.161	0.112	0.137	0.384	0.647	0.779	0.793	0.794	0.741	0.611	0.345

The x-coordinates are reported in seconds, and the y-coordinates are shown in meters, all rounded to the nearest thousandth. The chart gives you a subset of points from the scatterplot at the right, which shows the distance from the Slinky spring toy to the sensor at various times.

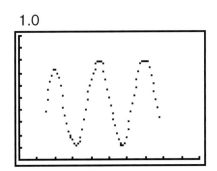

1.0

Enter the points from the chart into your calculator. You will use them to find a function that models the motion of the Slinky spring toy over the time interval in this data set. Start with the function $y = \cos x$ to model the position of the Slinky spring toy.

(Alternatively, you can collect your own data by using a motion sensor and a Slinky spring toy. Place the motion sensor on the floor, and allow the Slinky spring toy to oscillate up and down while someone holds one end of the toy at a fixed height above the sensor. Measure time in seconds, and measure the distances between the motion sensor and the oscillating end of the Slinky toy in meters. Enter the data that you collect into a chart like that above and use them as described.)

1. The x-coordinates of two consecutive relative minimum points are 1.591 and 2.838. What should you use for the period of the function that will model these data?

2. Two relative consecutive maximum points are (2.236, 0.793) and (3.526, 0.794). What should you use as the amplitude of the function that will model these data?

Name _____

3. What are the period and amplitude of the function $y = \cos x$? (Use radian measure.)

4. The first step in getting the two graphs to match is to decide how much you need to stretch or shrink the $y = \cos x$ graph horizontally so that the periods match. *Hint:* By what would you multiply the period of $y = \cos x$ to get the period found in number 1?

5. Next, decide how much you need to stretch or shrink the $y = \cos x$ graph vertically so that the amplitudes match. *Hint:* By what would you multiply the amplitude of $y = \cos x$ to obtain the amplitude that you found in number 2?

6. Starting with the cosine function, complete the connection diagram by using the scale change transformation suggested by numbers 4 and 5.

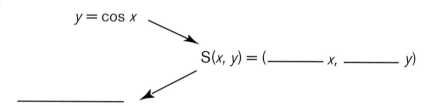

7. Where would the "midline" of the data set be?

8. The function that you found after the scale change in number 6 has the same period and amplitude as the graph of the data set. However, it reaches a maximum at $x = 0$ and has $y = 0$ as its midline. Find a translation of this function with a maximum value and midline that match the maximum value and midline of the data set. Complete the connection diagram at the right to find a function that models the data set.

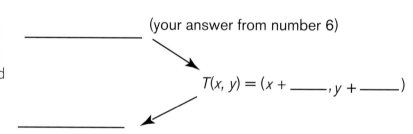

9. Check your final answer by entering the function into your calculator. How well does it fit the given points?

Sum Squares

Name _____

Line 'Em Up–Part 1

Do you remember how to find the vertex of a quadratic function of the form $f(x) = ax^2 + bx + c$? You can also use lines through the origin to estimate the y-values of points in a scatterplot.

1. *a.* On your calculator, create a graph of the function $y = 5x^2 - 40x + 128$ in a window that contains the vertex of the function. Use the trace option to find the coordinates of the vertex. What is the minimum value of this function? Does the function have any x-intercepts?

Vertex _____

Minimum value of y _____

x-intercepts _____

b. The following graphs show quadratic functions with two x-intercepts—that is, points where the graphs cross the x-axis. For each graph, explain how to find the x-coordinate of the vertex in terms of the x-intercepts.

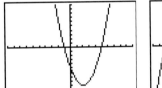 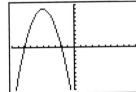

c. Recall that if a quadratic function $y = ax^2 + bx + c$ has two x-intercepts, these intercepts $(x_1$ and $x_2)$ are given by the quadratic formula:

$$x_1 = \frac{-b}{2a} - \frac{\sqrt{b^2 - 4ac}}{2a} \quad \text{and} \quad x_2 = \frac{-b}{2a} + \frac{\sqrt{b^2 - 4ac}}{2a}.$$

Find an expression for the x-coordinate of the vertex of such a quadratic function:

$$x_{vertex} = \underline{\hspace{3cm}}$$

d. You can translate any quadratic function vertically (up or down) so that it has two x-intercepts. Suppose that you translate the quadratic $y = ax^2 + bx + c$ vertically by k units so that it has two x-intercepts. Complete the connection diagram by showing the resulting quadratic function and x_{vertex}.

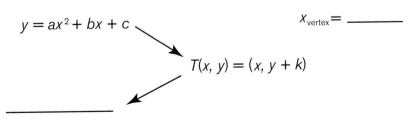

$y = ax^2 + bx + c$

$x_{vertex} = \underline{\hspace{1.5cm}}$

$T(x, y) = (x, y + k)$

Sum Squares (continued)

Name _____

e. What general conclusion can you draw about the x-coordinate of the vertex of any quadratic function of the form $y = ax^2 + bx + c$?

Does your answer in 1(a) fit this conclusion?

2. Consider the following sample data set and scatterplot of the xy-data:

x	y	$Y = 2x$	$(y - Y)^2$
−5	−1	−10	81
−2	−3	−4	1
3	0	6	36
4	4	8	16

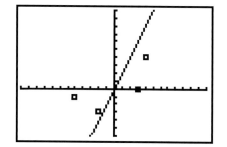

Statisticians use lines of best fit to represent ordered-pair data. Suppose that a statistician has selected the line $Y = 2x$ to represent the y-values in the data set. For each x-value in the data set, the difference between its y-value and the corresponding y-value on the line is called the *residual* and measures the deviation of the y-value predicted by the line from the y-value in the data set. Statisticians use the sum of the squares of all the residuals for a data set to decide how well a line "fits" the set, compared with other lines.

With the sample data set and the line $Y = 2x$, the sum of the squares of the residuals is $(-1 - (-10))^2 + (-3 - (-4))^2 + (0 - 6)^2 + (4 - 8)^2$, or $81 + 1 + 36 + 16$, or 134. Complete (a), (b), and (c) below to find the line through the origin that best fits the sample data—in other words, the line $Y = mx$ that minimizes the sum of the squares of the residuals.

a. Fill in the following chart by entering expressions for the squared residuals corresponding to each x-value.

x	y	$Y = mx$	$(y - Y)^2$
−5	−1	−5m	
−2	−3	−2m	
3	0	3m	
4	4	4m	

Navigating through Mathematical Connections in Grades 9–12

Sum Squares (continued)

Name _____

b. Add the expressions for the squared residuals in (*a*), and simplify the sum of the squares to an expression of the form $am^2 + bm + c$.

c. Use the results in number 1 to find the value of *m* that minimizes the quadratic expression in 2(*b*).

Line of best fit: $Y =$ ____x

Find the Line

Name _____

Line 'Em Up–Part 2

You can find a line through a set of data that minimizes the sum of the squares of the residuals. You can also use transformations to discover how to calculate lines of best fit for sets of data.

1. The scatterplot shows the points whose x- and y-coordinates appear in the chart below it.

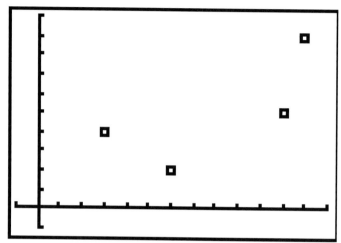

x	y	$Y = mx + b$	$(y - Y)^2$
3	4		
6	2		
11	5		
12	9		

In the scatterplot, draw a line that you think best fits the data. Use two points on your line to determine its equation, then complete the chart and calculate the sum of the squares of the residuals.

Equation of your line _____

Sum of squares of residuals _____

2. Let $\bar{x}$ be the mean of the x-values in the chart in number 1, and let $\bar{y}$ be the mean of the y-values. Plot the point $(\bar{x}, \bar{y})$ on the scatterplot in number 1. The point $(\bar{x}, \bar{y})$ is called the *centroid* of the data in the scatterplot. How close is $(\bar{x}, \bar{y})$ to the line that you guessed? Compare your result with the results obtained by others in your class.

Navigating through Mathematical Connections in Grades 9–12

Find the Line (continued)

Name _____

3. The centroid of any finite set of ordered pairs lies on the line of best fit for the ordered pairs. Do your results in number 2 support this general claim? Explain your answer.

4. Translate the graph in number 1, including the line that you guessed, to move $(\bar{x}, \bar{y})$ to the origin. Create a list of the transformed points, and complete the connection diagram to find the equation for the image of your line.

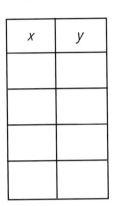

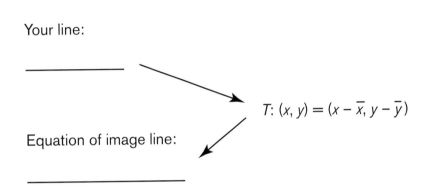

Your line:

_____

Equation of image line:

_____

$T: (x, y) = (x - \bar{x}, y - \bar{y})$

5. Find the sum of the squares of the residuals for the image line and the four points in the transformed data set. How does the sum compare with the sum that you found in number 1?

6. Explain why the sum of squares of the residuals is not affected when a data set and a line are translated in the plane.

7. Suppose that a data set D and its line of best fit, L, are translated in the plane. Explain why the image, L', of the line of best fit is the line of best fit for the transformed data.

8. Suppose that a data set is translated in the plane so that its centroid $(\bar{x}, \bar{y})$ is translated to the origin (0, 0). Explain why the line of best fit of the translated data set passes through the origin.

Name _____

9. Take a look back at the data set in number 2 of "Sum Squares" (part 1), and then look again at your transformed data set in number 4 here. Note that your transformed data set here is the same as that set. The line of best fit for the transformed data set here is therefore the line that you found there. Now use that line of best fit to find the line of best fit for the data set that appears in number 1 above. (*Hint:* Use an appropriate translation of that line to find the line of best fit for the data set in number1.)

10. Use your calculator's regression options to find the regression line for the data in number 1, and compare it with your answer in number 8.

11. Review the steps in "Sum Squares" and "Find the Line," and describe a method for finding the line of best fit for the following points: $\{(2, 3), (-3, 5), (4, 4)\}$.

Tiles in a Row

Name _____

In a particular mosaic design, colored tiles surround white square tiles, as shown below. Rows can have different numbers of white square tiles. The first example shows a row with 2 white square tiles surrounded by colored tiles. The second example shows 3 white square tiles surrounded by colored tiles.

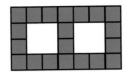 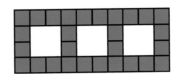

1. Using grid paper, draw a row in which colored tiles surround 4 white square tiles. Draw another row in which colored tiles surround 5 white square tiles. (The white tiles should be in a row, and each should have a side length equal to the side length of 2 colored tiles.)

2. Find a way to determine the number of colored tiles in each row without actually counting them all. Explain your method.

3. Use your method to determine the number of colored tiles in a row with 6 white square tiles. Try to determine this number without drawing a picture, but after you have an answer, draw a picture to verify that your answer is correct.

4. Use your method to determine how many colored tiles are in a row with 10 white square tiles. Write the exact sequence of steps and the operations that you used in calculating the number of colored tiles.

5. Suppose that a row will have *N* white square tiles. Rewrite your sequence of steps and operations in number 4, but use the variable *N* wherever you used the number 10. Write a formula that summarizes the results.

6. How many white tiles are in a row if 116 colored tiles will complete the pattern?

Constructing a Tape

Name _____

Measurement in the Round—Part 1

Your teacher has given you a can and a strip of paper or fabric to use to make a tape for measuring angles in radians. Your unit—that is, the length you will use as 1—will be the radius of the can. The length measurements that you make with your tape will indicate how many times the radius of your can fits into the length that you are measuring.

1. Place your can in the center of a piece of paper, and trace its circumference on the paper.

2. Find the center of the circle by folding your paper or by using a compass and a straightedge. Describe your method.

3. Explain why your method for finding the center of a circle works.

4. With a straightedge, draw a radius of the circle. Place one end of your tape on the center of the circle, and put a mark where the tape reaches the end of the radius. Place a 1 at that mark, since it measures one radius.

5. Use your radius again, and mark a 2 on your tape. Keep marking unit lengths after 2 along the tape until no room is left for another unit.

6. Your tape is beginning to look like a number line. Since you will use it as a measuring tape, mark more points and label them. Divide the units on your tape into halves and mark them

   $$\frac{1}{2}, \quad 1\frac{1}{2}, \quad 2\frac{1}{2}, \quad ....$$

   Describe how you can mark and label these points accurately without using a ruler.

7. Use your measuring tape to find the circumference of your can. Mark the point on your ruler that corresponds to the circumference of your can. What number might you use to label this point on your tape? Explain your answer.

Constructing a Tape (continued)

Name _____

8. Explain how to find the location of π on your measuring tape.

9. Divide the units on your measuring tape into fifths. You do not need to label the marks that you place on the edge of your tape. Describe how you can accurately divide the units into fifths without using a ruler.

Measuring Angles

Name _____

Measurement in the Round—Part 2

You can use your can to create a "unit circle" and your measuring tape to measure an arc, and in this way, you can find the "radian measure" for the directed angle corresponding to it.

1. In the center of a blank piece of paper, use a compass to draw a circle whose radius is the same as the unit on the measuring tape that you made in "Constructing a Tape." Draw a pair of perpendicular lines, one horizontal and one vertical, that intersect at the center of your circle. Label the lines *x* and *y* to indicate an *x-y* coordinate system. The circle is the unit circle of the coordinate system. The circumference of the can that you used for creating your measuring tape should closely fit your unit circle.

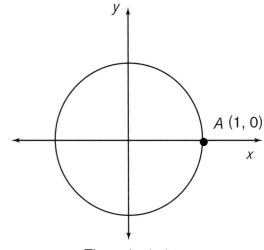

The unit circle

    Mark the intersection of the circle with the positive *x*-axis as the point *A*(1, 0), as shown in the figure.

2. A *directed angle in standard position* has its vertex at (0, 0) and one of its sides, called the *initial side,* on the positive *x*-axis. Its other side is called the *terminal side.* The names of the sides depict the angle as a rotation around the vertex that moves the initial side to the terminal side of the angle. The size of the rotation determines the measure of the angle. Draw an acute angle in standard position as shown at the right. Use your tape to measure the length of the arc of the rotation represented by the angle. Estimate the length to the nearest tenth. This measurement is the *radian* measure of the angle, since it tells how many times the radius of the circle fits into the arc of rotation corresponding to the angle.

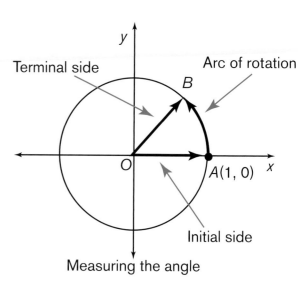

Measuring the angle

    Hint: To measure the angle of the rotation that moves the initial side to the terminal side, place your can over the unit circle. With the 0 of the measuring tape starting at *A*(1, 0), wrap the tape around the can in the direction of the rotation.

3. *a.* Find the radian measure of the directed angle whose arc of rotation corresponds to the upper half of the unit circle.

Measuring Angles (continued)

Name _____

b. Find the radian measure of the directed angle whose arc of rotation corresponds to the fourth of the unit circle that is contained in the first quadrant.

c. Find the radian measure of the directed angle whose arc of rotation corresponds to the entire unit circle.

d. Explain your answers in 3 (a), (b), and (c).

4. Place the 0 mark on your measuring tape at the point $A(1, 0)$, and wrap the tape around the unit circle in a counterclockwise direction. Then draw the directed angles with the following radian measures:
   a. 1 radian

   b. 2 radians

   c. 1.5 radians

   d. 5 radians

   e. 10 radians

5. Compare your answers in number 4 with the answers obtained by others in your class. Explain why the angles constructed by a person who used a different-sized can for his or her unit circle appear to be congruent to the angles that you drew.

Measuring Angles (continued)

Name _____

6. *a.* Imagine your measuring tape to be a number line that extends to infinity in both the positive and negative directions. If you wrapped the positive part of this number line around the unit circle in a counterclockwise direction, as in number 4, and wrapped the negative part of the number line around the unit circle in a clockwise direction, what radian measures would be associated with the directed angles, in standard position, shown at the right?

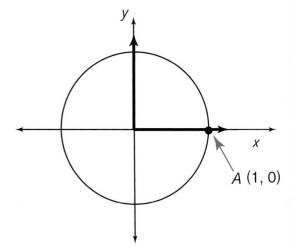

A (1, 0)

  b. Describe the rotations represented by directed angles with negative radian measures, as well as the rotations represented by directed angles with positive radian measures.

Defining Trigonometric Functions

You can find the trigonometric functions of an angle θ by placing the angle in standard position, with its vertex at the center of the unit circle and its initial ray along the positive x-axis, as shown in the following diagram. The terminal ray of the angle intersects the circle at a point (x, y). The sine of θ is y, and the cosine of θ is x.

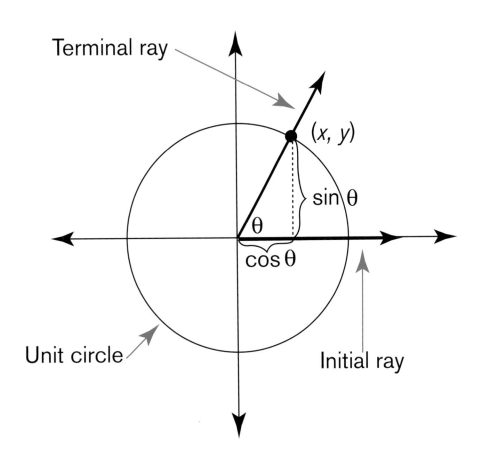

You can find the tangent of an angle α by placing the angle in standard position, drawing the line tangent to the circle through *A*(1, 0), and finding the point *T* where it intersects the line containing the terminal side of the angle. The tangent is the *y*-coordinate of *T*.

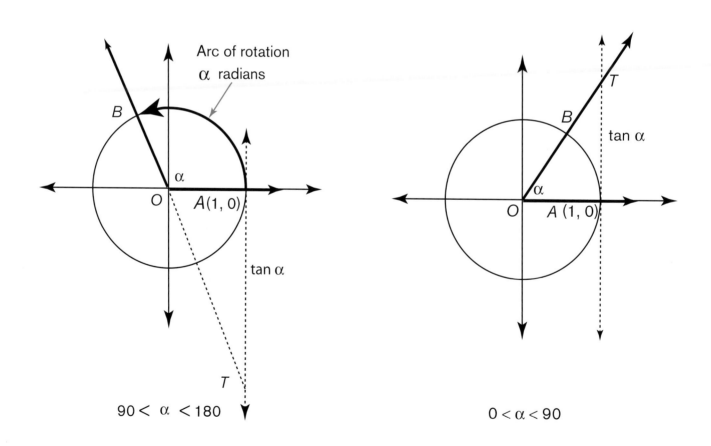

Graphing Circular Functions

Name _____

Measurement in the Round—Part 3

The measuring tape that you made in "Constructing a Tape" represents not only lengths whose units are the radius of your can but also directed angle measures of the various arcs of the unit circle that you traced from the can. You can use your tape along with your coordinate system and unit circle from "Measuring Angles" to represent the sine, cosine, and tangent functions as lengths in a new graph.

1. On grid paper, create an *x*-*y* coordinate system with the *x*-axis scaled in half-units from −4 to 4. For each value marked on the *x*-axis, plot the sine of the angle whose radian measure corresponds to that value. *Hint:* To find the sine value corresponding to *x* = 2, for example, first find the angle ∠*AOB* corresponding to the arc of rotation whose measure is 2 radians on the unit circle, as in the diagram at the left.

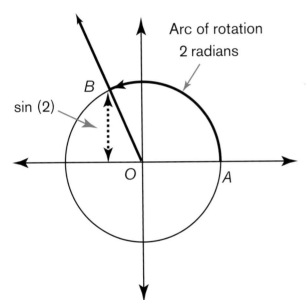

Then use your tape to determine the *y*-coordinate of the point *B*, where the angle intersects the unit circle. This *y*-coordinate is the sine of 2 radians, or sin (2). Draw the point on your graph with *x*-coordinate 2 and *y*-coordinate sin (2), as shown.

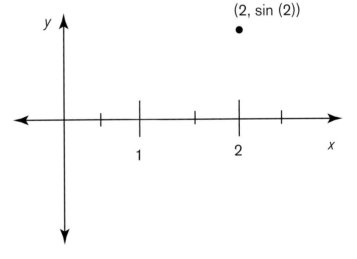

Repeat this process for each of the marked points on the *x*-axis. You will then have an outline of the graph of the sine function between −4 and 4.

2. On grid paper, draw a graph of the cosine function between −4 and 4. Remember that the cosine of an angle is the *x*-coordinate of the point of intersection of the angle with the unit circle.

Graphing Circular Functions (continued)

Name _____

3. As shown in the graph below, the tangent of the angle ∠AOB associated with the arc is the distance from *A,* the point at (1, 0) on the unit circle, to *T*, the intersection of the tangent to the circle at *A* with the (extended) terminal side of the angle. If *T* is below the *x*-axis, as it is in the graph, the tangent is negative. If *T* is above the *x*-axis, the tangent is positive. In short, the tangent is the *y*-coordinate of the point *T*.

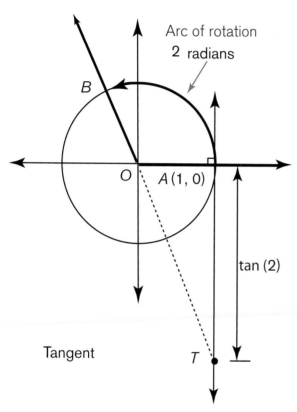

Use this definition of the tangent to graph the tangent function between −4 and 4. (*Note:* Some points may be difficult to graph.)

4. In the graph of the tangent function, there are points on the *x*-axis for which the tangent function is not defined. Identify these points on the graph that you made in number 3. Describe the behavior of the graph for values of *x* near these points.

5. Compare your work in numbers 1–3 with that of others in your class. Explain how the graphs constructed by students who used different-sized cans are the same as yours and how they differ.

Navigating through Mathematical Connections in Grades 9–12

Interpreting Transit Graphs

The graph below is a *transit graph.* Transit graphs are useful in plotting travel that occurs in two directions on a route containing one or more segments over which the traffic flow must be one-way.

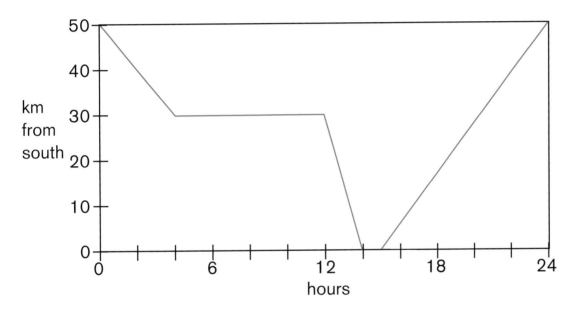

The line with three segments beginning at the left edge of the graph represents a southbound ship that enters a canal at the 0-hour mark. It travels at 5 km/hr and docks at the (4 hr, 30 km) mark for 8 hours before finishing its journey at a rate of 15 km/hr. One hour after the first ship arrives at the south end of the canal, a northbound ship departs at 50/9, or about 5.6, km/hr.

The transit graph below depicts two southbound convoys, a northbound ship that pauses at the 20-km mark for an hour before returning to the south end of the canal, and (at the right edge) two ships colliding at the 30-km mark.

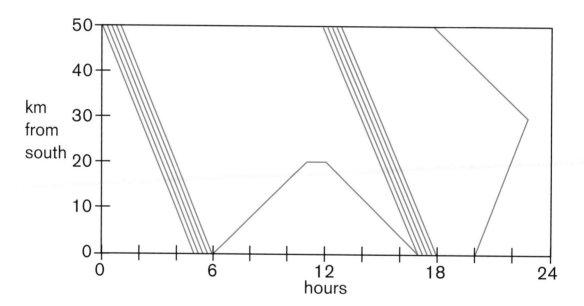

What would people standing at the 10-km mark on the canal observe, and when would they observe it?

The transit graph below depicts two convoys of ships passing each other safely in a "bypass zone."

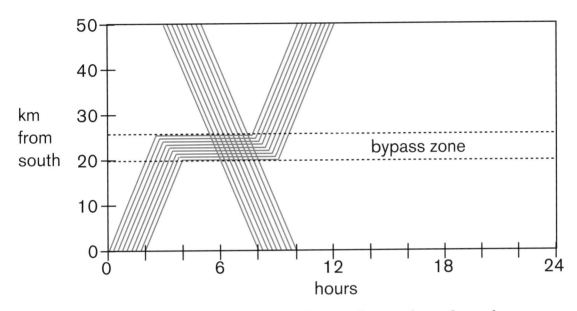

The northbound ships arrive first in the bypass zone and anchor (note the horizontal segments of their graphs) while the southbound ships pass through the bypass zone without stopping. The northbound ships then resume their travel and maintain a safety spacing of 15 minutes. *Note:* If ships depart 15 minutes apart—that is, if they have a "safety spacing" of 15 minutes—9 ships will occupy 2 hours of time between the first and last ship.

Transit graphs show a bypass zone with docking facilities as a horizontal band (labeled in the graph above).

Graphs That Tell Stories

Name _____

Transit Graphs—Part 1

You can use a *transit graph* to plot travel that occurs in two directions on a route but must be one-way on a narrow section of the route, such as a canal. You can create and interpret transit graphs for various scenarios. Keep in mind the following important concepts of transit graphs:

- Slope represents velocity, and positive and negative slopes represent speeds in opposite directions.

- A horizontal line indicates a ship at rest.

- A vertical line is meaningless because a ship cannot be in more than one place at one time and because the velocity (slope) is undefined for vertical lines.

- Although slanted lines appear on the graph, all movement is in fact along the line defined by the canal or a ship's route of travel; the orientation of the segments on the graph does not indicate a ship's movement.

Begin by describing the movement of the ships depicted on the following transit graphs. Determine times, distances, and speeds of significance.

1. Transit graph 1

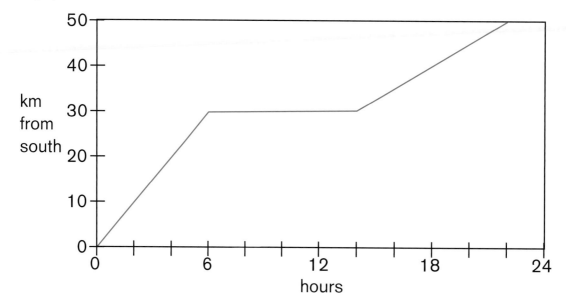

Navigating through Mathematical Connections in Grades 9–12

Graphs That Tell Stories (continued)

Name _____

2. Transit graph 2

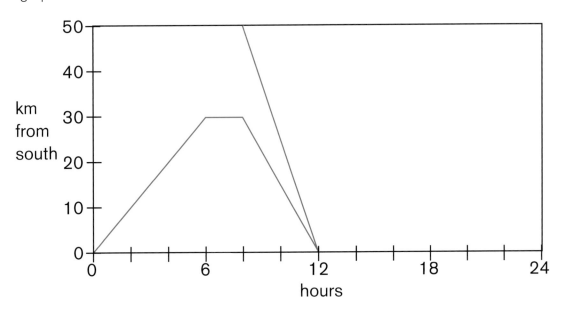

3. Transit graph 3

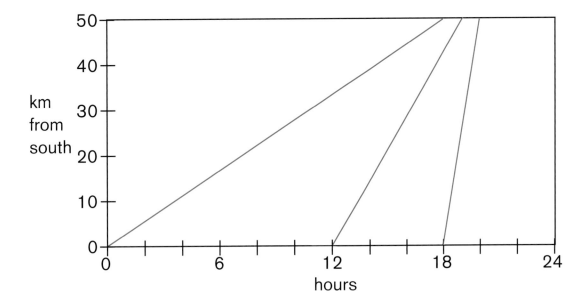

Graphs That Tell Stories (continued)

Name _____

4. Transit graph 4

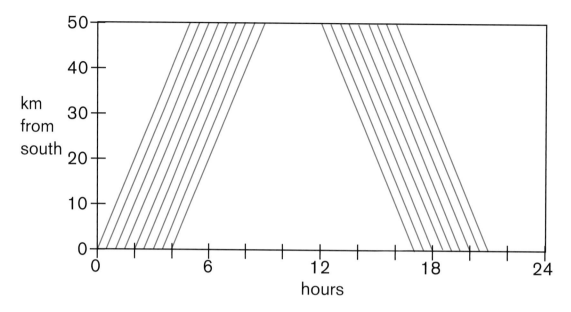

5. Assume that a canal has the same characteristics as the canals shown in numbers 1–4. Create transit graphs that depict each of the following situations.

a. A ship enters the north end of the canal at the 4-hr mark and travels at a rate of 15 km/hr through the canal without stopping. As soon as the ship arrives at the south end of the canal, a northbound ship, which is traveling at a rate of 25 km/hr, departs. Four more northbound ships follow this one, each separated by 30 minutes from the one ahead of it.

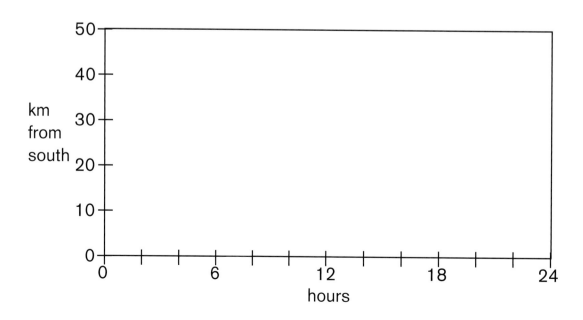

Navigating through Mathematical Connections in Grades 9–12

Name _____

b. A ship enters the south end of the canal at the 2-hr mark and travels for 3 hours at 10 km/hr before developing engine trouble. It comes to a halt for 4 hours while the engine is repaired. The ship then continues on its way north at 5 km/hr. As soon as the ship arrives at the north end of the canal, a southbound ship begins its journey and travels through the canal without mishap at 5 km/hr.

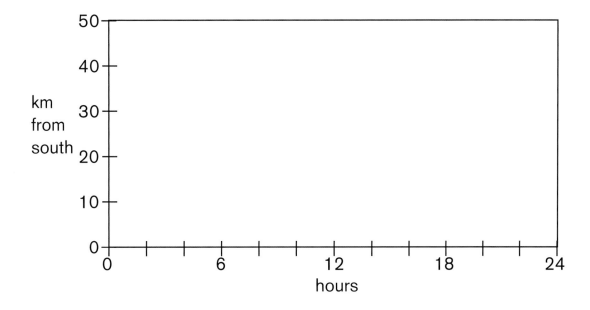

Creating Optimal Schedules

Name _____

Transit Graphs—Part 2

Consider the situations described in numbers 1, 2, and 4 below. Create a transit graph for each situation. Your transit graph should reflect the constraints of the situation and should allow as many ships as possible to pass through the canal in the time specified.

1. All ships travel at 10 km/hr. Ships headed in the same direction must maintain a "safety spacing" of 15 minutes between ships. Within every 24-hour cycle, the number of northbound ships must equal the number of southbound ships.

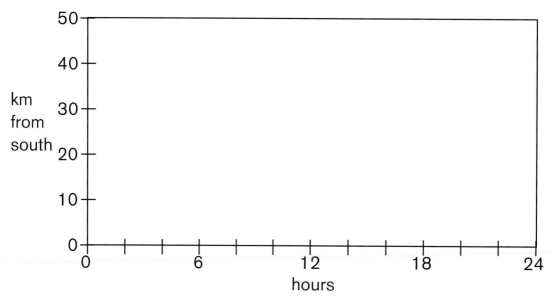

2. All ships travel at 10 km/hr. Ships headed in the same direction must maintain a safety spacing of 15 minutes between ships. Within every 48-hour cycle, the number of northbound ships must equal the number of southbound ships.

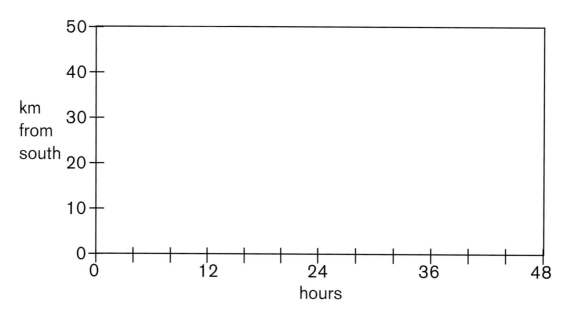

Navigating through Mathematical Connections in Grades 9–12

Creating Optimal Schedules (continued)

Name _____

3. Compare the efficiency of the schedules that you produced in numbers 1 and 2 by calculating the ratio of ships per hour that travel through the canal over the course of one complete cycle. What can you conclude about the relationship between the length and the efficiency of the cycles?

4. All ships travel at 10 km/hr. Ships headed in the same direction must maintain a safety spacing of 15 minutes between ships. A "bypass zone," at which 30 ships can dock, is located between the 30- and 35-mile marks. Northbound ships, which are often fully loaded, cannot dock but must complete their trips through the canal without stopping. Ships can pass safely only if the southbound ships are docked in the bypass zone, as indicated by horizontal line segments. In every 24-hour cycle, the number of northbound ships must equal the number of southbound ships.

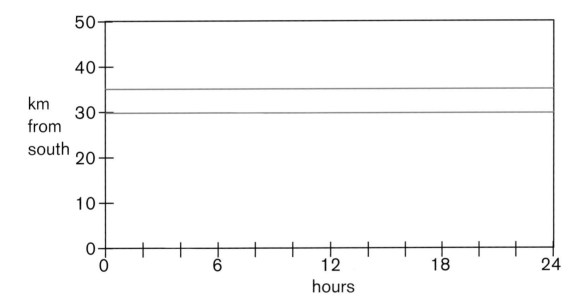

Selecting a Location

Name _____

Quick Response Time—Part 1

Three small towns are on a rural highway whose milepost numbers increase as one travels east. Littleton is at milepost 5, Smallsville is at milepost 17, and Tinytown is at milepost 20. The towns are pooling their funds to build a fire station. The planners have decided that the station should be at the point along the highway where the average response time to any of the towns is the least. Since the time from when a fire alarm sounds to the time when the fire truck enters the highway is the same for any fire, the response time depends primarily on the distance along the highway that the truck must travel to reach the fire. The planners' task is thus to find the point on the highway from which the sum of the distances to the three towns is the smallest.

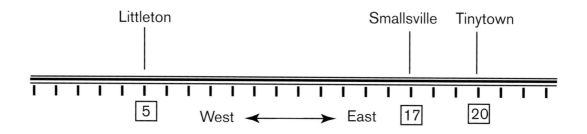

1. Why is the point on the highway from which the sum of the distances to the three towns is the least also the point from which the average response time is the shortest? What assumptions do you make in your explanation?

2. Suppose that the planners decide to locate the fire station at milepost 13.

   a. How far will the fire station be from each of the three towns?

   b. What will the total distance be from the fire station to the three towns?

3. Suppose that decimal numbers designate the points between the mileposts, as on a number line, so that the point halfway between mileposts 13 and 14 is 13.5, for example. What will be the total distance from the fire station to the three towns if the fire station is at the point 16.5?

Selecting a Location (continued)

Name _____

4. *a.* Find the location that is "best," in the sense that it minimizes the total distance to the three towns.

   b. How can you convince someone that the location you have selected is the best one?

5. Suppose that the three towns are at mileposts 55, 59, and 70. Find the best location for the fire station, and briefly describe how you would locate the fire station for any three towns along this highway.

6. Suppose that the three towns are at mileposts 5, 17, and 20, and that a fourth town, at milepost 0, wants to join them in building the fire station.

   a. Where should the towns locate the fire station?

   b. Does the procedure that you outlined in number 5 work for four towns?

7. *a.* Outline a procedure to find the best location of a fire station for any set of four towns.

   b. Make up an example that tests your procedure.

8. The towns of Bug Crossing and Punyberg are located at mileposts 0 and 23, respectively. Suppose that they join Littleton, Smallsville, and Tinytown (located as in the original scenario) in the fire station project.

   a. Where should the towns situate the fire station?

   b. Explain a general method for determining the best location of a fire station for any number of towns on the highway.

   c. How could you convince someone that this method works?

Name _____

9. Suppose that the planners propose the location that you identified in number 8. The citizens of Bug Crossing and Littleton review the proposal and decide that it treats them unfairly. They assert that the planners have made a mistake in deciding that the "best" location is the one that minimizes the average response time to the towns.

    a. If you were the representative from Bug Crossing, how would you argue your case before the planning board?

    b. What alternative method would you suggest for a fairer location?

Generalizing Results

Name _____

Quick Response Time—Part 2

In part 1, "Selecting a Location, you determined the best location for a fire station serving three small towns—Littleton, Smallsville, and Tinytown.

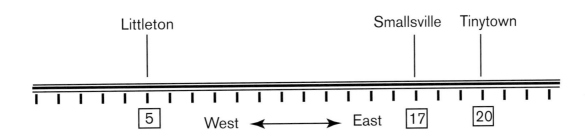

Functions and graphs can provide a new perspective on possible locations for the fire station.

1. In number 4 in "Selecting a Location," you found the "best" location for the fire station—that is, the location that minimizes the sum of the distances from three towns. To demonstrate that your solution to that problem is correct, you can use algebra to analyze all the possible locations. Assume that the fire station is located at point x, and write an expression for its distance from each of the towns.

Town	Distance to Fire Station
Littleton	
Smallsville	
Tinytown	

2. Write a function that gives the total distance from the fire station to the original three towns in terms of x, the location of the fire station.

3. *a.* Graph your function on a graphing calculator, and find the value of x that minimizes the total distance.

   b. Does this value agree with your solution in number 4 in "Selecting a Location"?

Generalizing Results (continued)

Name _____

4. From a statistical point of view, the best location of the fire station for the original three towns is the

   _____ of the set {5, 17, 20}.

5. Include the town of Bug Crossing, at milepost 0, in your calculations. Modify your function from number 2, and graph the new function on a graphing calculator. Does your new graph support your response in number 6 in "Selecting a Location"?

6. Include the town of Punyberg, at milepost 23, in your calculations. Modify your function from number 5, and graph the new function on a graphing calculator. Does your new graph support your response in number 8 in "Selecting a Location"?

7. On the basis of your graphs, what general conclusions can you make about the best location for the fire station?

The Fairest of Them All

Name _____

Quick Response Time—Part 3

Recall that in part 1, you supposed that the residents of Bug Crossing and Littleton do not like the location that the planners have proposed for the fire station by applying the criterion of minimum response time. Suppose that the residents of those two cities propose that the station be closer to the "center" of the stretch of highway that connects the five towns. Imagine that the planners in fact receive three proposals for a location that is more "central" than the location determined on the basis of minimum response time. Your task is to analyze each proposal.

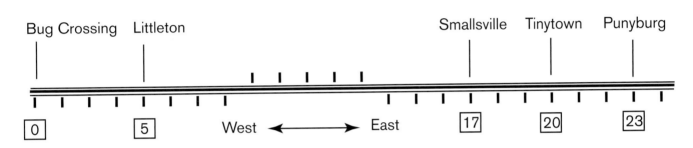

1. The citizens of Bug Crossing propose that the location exactly halfway between Bug Crossing and Punyberg be recognized as the center and therefore the fairest place to locate the fire station.

   a. Identify this location on the highway, and compute the total distance from it to the five towns.

   b. Why do the citizens of Bug Crossing favor this plan, and how do you think the residents of the other towns will respond? Give reasons for your answers.

2. The citizens of Tinytown believe that the original plan favors the three cities on the east and that Bug Crossing's plan favors the two cities on the west. The citizens of Tinytown recommend that the center be the point on the highway from which the total of the distances to the cities on the west equals the total of the distances to the cities on the east.

   a. Locate this point on the highway, and compute its total distance from the five towns.

   b. Describe an efficient method for locating this point.

Name _____

3. *a.* If *x* is the location of the fire station, explain why solving the following equation provides the location in Tinytown's proposal in number 2:

$$(x - 0) + (x - 5) + (x - 17) + (x - 20) + (x - 23) = 0.$$

    b. Assume that the five towns are at points *a, b, c, d,* and *e* on the highway. Find an equation that uses Tinytown's criterion to find the center of these towns, and solve it. What general conclusion can you make about Tinytown's criterion?

4. Although the residents of Littleton sympathize with the plight of Bug Crossing, they do not like the emphasis on the differences between the east and west distances. The residents of Littleton propose that the standard deviation of the towns' distances from the fire station be minimized. This method would minimize the "spread" in the distance data, thereby identifying a location that is fairer for everyone. The residents of Littleton contend that minimizing the sum of the squares of the distances of towns to the fire station will give a location that satisfies their criterion.

    a. Try various locations for the fire station, and compute the sums of the squared distances from the five towns to the fire station.

    b. When you minimized the sum of the distances in number 4 of "Selecting a Location," the best location for the fire station was milepost 17, or Smallsville. Is Smallsville the best location if you are trying to minimize the sum of the squares of the distances?

    c. What is the best location for the fire station if you want to minimize the sum of the squares of the distances? How could you persuade someone that your location is best?

The Fairest of Them All (continued)

Name _____

5. To convince someone that the location that you found in number 4 is best, you can use algebra to analyze all the possible locations. Assume that the fire station is located at point *x,* and enter expressions in the chart below for its squared distance from each of the towns.

Town	Distance to Fire Station
Bug Crossing	
Littleton	
Smallsville	
Tinytown	
Punyberg	

6. *a.* Write a function that gives the total of the squared distances from the five towns to the fire station in terms of *x,* the milepost of the fire station.

    b. Graph your function on a graphing calculator, and find the value of *x* that minimizes the sum of the squared distances. How does this location compare with the other proposed locations? What general conclusions can you make about Littleton's criterion?

The Double-Dare Situation

Name _____

Double-Dare—Part 1

In some games, such as backgammon, when player A is ahead, she or he can "double" the other player, player B. When player B receives this challenge, he or she must either quit and give player A a point for winning or continue to play for a double score (two points). Since player B is behind and thus is more likely to lose, the key question is whether he or she stands to lose more *in the long run* by always choosing to continue to play on than by always choosing to quit in a double-dare situation. In other words, should player B *always* quit when player A doubles? Or should player B *always* play on?

Imagine that you are playing a game that you are losing. In fact, you know that your probability of losing is two-thirds and that your probability of winning is one-third. Your opponent doubles you. You must decide whether to quit, thereby letting your opponent win one point, or to play on for two points. What will you decide?

Double-Dare Simulation

Name _____

Double-Dare—Part 2

Imagine that you are playing a game and have reached a point at which you have a two-thirds chance of losing and a one-third chance of winning. Your opponent doubles you. Should you accept and play on, with the winner earning two points instead of one? Conduct a simulation to discover whether you are better off in the long run by quitting every time and giving your opponent one point (the "I quit" strategy), or by playing on every time in the hope of winning two points (the "play on" strategy).

1. Make an intuitive guess about whether you should quit or accept the double and play on. Circle one of the following options:

   "I quit" strategy   "Play on" strategy

2. Work with a partner to simulate what would happen if you played 30 games in which you received a double-dare challenge, and you used the "play on" strategy each time. To begin the simulation, put 2 red cubes and 1 yellow cube in a bag. Shake the bag well, and pull out a cube. If it is red, you lose 2 points. If it is yellow, you win 2 points. Return the cube to the bag, shake the bag, and draw again. To simulate 30 games, repeat the process 30 times. Use chart 1 to keep track of the number of times that you win, as well as the points that you win or lose.

Chart 1— "Play On" Strategy

Game	Win or Lose (W/L)	Points Won	Points Lost	Game	Win or Lose (W/L)	Points Won	Points Lost
1				16			
2				17			
3				18			
4				19			
5				20			
6				21			
7				22			
8				23			
9				24			
10				25			
11				26			
12				27			
13				28			
14				29			
15				30			

Double-Dare Simulation (continued)

Name _____

When you finish, record your results for the "play on" strategy in row 1 of chart 2:

Chart 2—Cumulative Results from 30 Games

Strategy	Number of Games Won	Number of Games Lost	Number of Points Won	Number of Points Lost	Total Score
"Play on"					
"I quit"					

3. Next, assume that you play 30 games and use the "I quit" strategy each time. Record your results in row 2 of chart 2 above.

   a. How many points do you expect to lose by the end of the 30 games?

   b. Which strategy, the "I quit" strategy or the "play on" strategy, gives you a better score?

4. When someone follows a specific strategy, the average score per game in the long run is called the "expected value" of the strategy.

   a. What is your expected value if you consistently use the "I quit" strategy?

   b. Use the results of your simulation to estimate your expected value if you consistently use the "play on" strategy.

   c. Which expected value is better for you?

Double-Dare Theory

Name _____

Double-Dare—Part 3

From your simulation and those of your classmates, you have probably concluded that accepting a double and playing on when you have a two-thirds probability of losing is a better strategy than quitting. You lose in the long run with both strategies, but it looks as though you lose less by playing on. How can you be sure? A simulation provides only an estimate of an expected value, or the average value in the long run. What does the theory of probability say?

1. Assume that you use the "I quit" strategy in 30 games. What is your expected value—that is, the average number of points that you are likely to earn in a game? Explain your reasoning.

2. Assume that you use the "play on" strategy in 30 games. On a sheet of grid paper, make a rectangle containing 30 squares arranged in 10 rows, with 3 columns of squares in each row. Let each square represent 1 of the 30 games. Shade the squares that represent the games that you expect to lose if the probability of losing is two-thirds. Count each shaded square as −2 points and each unshaded square as +2 points, and calculate the total number of points that you have at the end of the 30 games. Divide this point total by 30 to find the expected value for the "play on" strategy.

   a. Record the expected value that you found.

   b. Is your value close to the estimate that you made from your simulation?

3. From the expected values that you found in numbers 1 and 2, which strategy, "play on" or "I quit," is better in theory? Explain your reasoning.

4. Suppose that the number of games in number 2 is 75.
   a. What is the expected value?

   b. Does the number of games affect the outcome of the calculation? Explain.

Double-Dare Theory (continued)

Name _____

5. You have already found the expected values for both strategies when the probability of losing is two-thirds. Choose three other probabilities of losing, and find the expected values for each strategy. Record your results.

Probability of losing _____

Strategy	Expected Value
"Play on"	
"I quit"	

Probability of losing _____

Strategy	Expected Value
"Play on"	
"I quit"	

Probability of losing _____

Strategy	Expected Value
"Play on"	
"I quit"	

6. What happens to the expected value for the "I quit" strategy as the probability of losing increases?

7. What happens to the expected value for the "play on" strategy as the probability of losing increases? Explain why the expected value changes in that way.

8. With your partner and another pair of students, discuss the circumstances under which the "I quit" strategy is best. Under what circumstances is the "play on" strategy best? Record your conclusions.

Navigating through Mathematical Connections in Grades 9–12

Double-Dare with Algebra

Name _____

Double-Dare—Part 4

When the probability of losing is two-thirds, your expected value—your average score in the long run—is better if you play on than if you quit. In some cases where the probability of losing is higher than two-thirds, you have seen that the expected value is higher if you quit. A break-even point, at which the expected values for the "I quit" and the "play on" strategies are equal, exists in the probabilities. When the probability of losing equals that break-even point, neither strategy is better than the other. You can use algebra to determine the break-even point.

1. If you can find the break-even point—that is, the point at which the expected values for the two strategies are equal—you will know when to quit and when to accept a double-dare challenge. Explain why this statement is true.

2. To begin to find the break-even point, assume that you play 100 games and that the variable P is the probability of losing a game.

   a. In terms of P, what is the probability of winning a game?

   b. Assume that you use the "play on" strategy for 100 games. Express the number of games that you expect to win in terms of P.

   c. In terms of P, how many points do you expect to win for those 100 games?

   d. In terms of P, how many of the 100 games do you expect to lose?

   e. In terms of P, how many points do you expect to lose for those games?

   f. When you combine your expected wins and losses, what total score do you expect for the 100 games if you use the "play on" strategy?

   g. What total score do you expect for the 100 games if you use the "I quit" strategy?

Double-Dare with Algebra

Name _____

3. Use your answers for numbers 2(f) and 2(g) to write an equation in terms of P that indicates when the expected score for the "play on" strategy equals the expected score for the "I quit" strategy. Find the break-even probability. That is, find the probability of losing when the expected value for both strategies is the same.

4. Write a complete plan that indicates when a player should quit and when a player should accept a double in a double-dare situation.

Measuring the Middle Pole

Name _____

Support Cables—Part 1

To ensure the safety of its trapeze artists, a circus secures its trapezes with a structure of interconnected poles, cables, and nets. The illustration shows a small portion of one such structure.

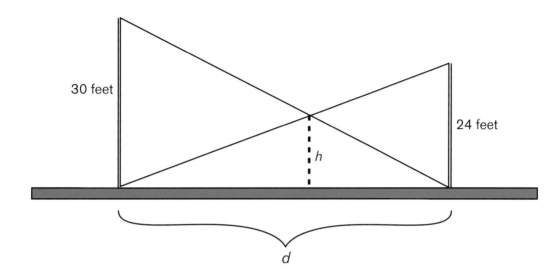

In this arrangement, support cables connect two poles—one 30 feet tall and the other 24 feet tall. A cable connects the top of each pole to the base of the opposite pole. A third pole secures the cables at the point where they intersect.

What is the height (h) of the middle pole? Does h depend on the distance (d) between the outer poles?

In this exploration, you will use grid paper to represent the problem and estimate the solution. Since the distance (d) between the two end poles is unknown, select different distances for d and determine the height, h, for each distance.

1. Select a scale for your drawing. What distance does each unit on your grid paper represent?

2. Suppose that $d = 40$ feet. On your grid paper, accurately represent this distance, the two end poles, the cables connecting the end poles, and the middle pole. Use your drawing and the grid lines on your paper to measure h. What is the height of the middle pole?

Name _____

3. Your teacher will give you a different value for *d.* Repeat the process from number 2, substituting your new value. What is the height of the third pole?

4. Compare your results with those of others in your class, and make a conjecture. Does the height of the middle pole depend on the distance between the outer poles? Explain your answer.

Interactive Measurement

Name _____

Support Cables–Part 2

To ensure the safety of its trapeze artists, a circus secures its trapezes with a structure of interconnected poles, cables, and nets. The illustration shows a small portion of one such structure.

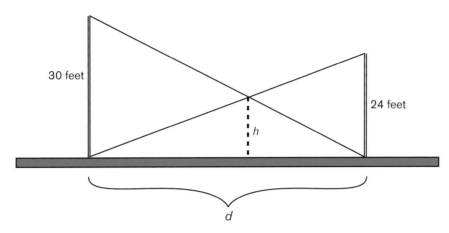

In this arrangement, support cables connect two poles—one 30 feet tall and the other 24 feet tall. A cable connects the top of each pole to the base of the opposite pole. A third pole secures the cables at the point where they intersect.

What is the height (h) of the middle pole? Does h depend on the distance (d) between the outer poles?

In this exploration, you will use the computer applet Support Cables to determine the solution to this problem. Since the distance (d) between the two end poles is unknown, select different distances for d and determine h for each distance.

Use the slider bars on the applet to set the height of the end poles at 30 feet and 24 feet. Use the slider bar to select five different values of d. In the following chart, record the value of h for each value of d.

d	h

Compare the values for h in your chart with those of two other students. Does the height, h, depend on the distance between the end poles? Explain.

Proving Your Conjecture

Name _____

Support Cables—Part 3

In parts 1 and 2, you discovered that the height of the middle pole is approximately 13 feet and does not depend on the distance between the end poles. You can use two different approaches—one with similar triangles and another with analytic geometry—to verify these conjectures.

Approach 1 (Similar Triangles)

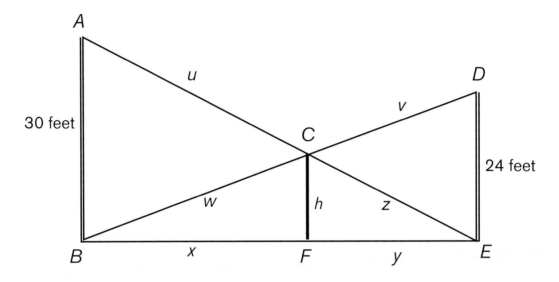

1. Identify all pairs of similar triangles in the figure. Assume that segments $\overline{AB}$, $\overline{CF}$, and $\overline{DE}$ in the figure are perpendicular to the base, $\overline{BE}$.

2. Explain why $\triangle ABC \sim \triangle EDC$, and list the proportions involving the ratios of their corresponding sides.

3. What is the ratio of x to y? Justify your answer.

4. Find a proportion that involves x, y, and h. Combine it with your answer to problem 3 to determine h. Does your solution depend on the length of the base $\overline{BE}$? Explain.

Proving Your Conjecture (continued)

Name _____

Approach 2 (Analytic Geometry)

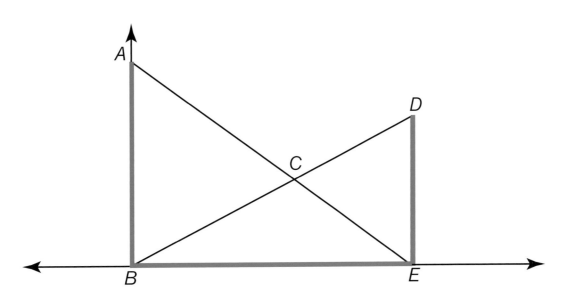

5. In the diagram, the length of $\overline{AB}$ is 30 feet, the length of $\overline{DE}$ is 24 feet, and the length of $\overline{BE}$ is *d*. Construct this diagram in the *xy*-coordinate plane so that *B* is at the point (0, 0) and *A* is at the point (0, 30). What are the coordinates of points *D* and *E*?

6. What is the equation of the line containing points *B* and *D*? What is the equation of the line containing points *A* and *E*?

7. Use the equations from number 6 to find the coordinates of point *C*.

8. Does the *y*-coordinate of point *C* depend on the length of $\overline{BE}$? Explain.

Is There a Better Way?

Name _____

Support Cables—Part 4

In part 3, you proved that the distance between the outer poles did not affect the height of the middle pole. This result suggests that there might be a way to prove that the height of the middle pole is $13\frac{1}{3}$ feet without introducing any variable other than *h*. Consider the following diagram.

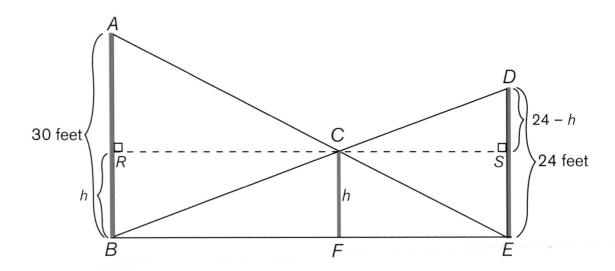

1. In part 3, you proved that $\triangle ABC \sim \triangle EDC$. Identify all pairs of corresponding segments in these two triangles. List only the pairs whose endpoints are labeled in the diagram above.

2. In simplest form, what is the ratio of each corresponding pair of segments in number 1?

3. Set up a proportion involving only one variable, *h* and use it to prove that $h = 13\frac{1}{3}$ feet.

4. Assume that the heights of the two outer poles are *p* and *q*. Modify your proportion in number 3 to find an expression for the height of the middle pole.

Navigating through Mathematical Connections in Grades 9–12

Solutions for the Blackline Masters

Solutions for "Breath by Breath"

Growing Balloons—Part 1

1–3. The table and graphs in the discussion of the activity in the text depict sample data relating the number of breaths and the circumference of a balloon. Values will vary, depending on the size and physical properties of the balloons that your students use and the consistency of the students' breathing as they inflate them. The power regression function $y = 21.54x^{0.37}$ (or $c = 21.54b^{0.37}$) fits the data points and the trend in the sample fairly well.

Solutions for "Take a Breath and Theorize"

Growing Balloons—Part 2:

You may need to guide some students through the algebraic manipulations that the activity requires.

1. $c = 2\pi r$, and $v = \dfrac{4}{3}\pi r^3$.

2. $r = \sqrt[3]{\dfrac{3v}{4\pi}}$.

3. $c = 2\pi \sqrt[3]{\dfrac{3v}{4\pi}}$.

4. $v = kb$, where k is a constant that depends on the volume of each breath.

5. $c = 2\pi \sqrt[3]{\dfrac{3kb}{4\pi}}$.

6. $c = 2\pi \sqrt[3]{\dfrac{3k}{4\pi}}\left(\sqrt[3]{b}\right) = \sqrt[3]{\dfrac{8\pi^3 3k}{4\pi}}\left(\sqrt[3]{b}\right) = \sqrt[3]{6\pi^2 k}\left(\sqrt[3]{b}\right)$.

7. The following data are samples are from table 1.1 in the text:

Number (b) of Breaths	$\sqrt[3]{\text{Number of Breaths}}$	Circumference (c) (cm)
1	1.00	21.0
2	1.26	28.5
3	1.44	32.5
4	1.59	37.0
5	1.71	39.0
6	1.82	41.5
7	1.91	43.0

Figure 1.5 in the text shows a scatterplot of the circumference versus the cube root of the number of breaths for the sample data.

8. The line $c = 22.5\sqrt[3]{b}$ fits the sample data well. We can find the slope of this line by using the data for breath 7 (1.91, 43) and the origin (0, 0): $m = (43 - 0)/(1.91 - 0) = 22.5$. Students' answers will vary.

9. The theoretical model $c = 22.5\sqrt[3]{b}$ is similar to the empirical model $c = 21.54b^{0.37}$ in both the leading coefficient and exponent.

Solutions for "Experimenting with a Dosage"

Healthy Dose—Part 1

Students' responses will vary. The table below shows data for an initial dose of 120 mg.

Time (hr)	Amount of Drug in the Body (mg)
0	120.00
4	108.00
8	97.20
12	87.48
16	78.73
20	70.86
24	63.77

1. *a* and *b*. Students should select initial doses between 40 mg and 600 mg. Those students who select a dose that is close to 40 mg will need to adjust their selection after filling in the chart. (For example, an initial dose of 50 mg will fall below the 40-mg threshold in less than 12 hours.

2. *a* and *b*. After completing the chart for a 24-hour period, students should describe the process. Most will describe a recursive strategy, in which the amount in row *n* is 0.9 of the amount in row *n* − 1.

3. *a–d*. For the sample data above, an initial dose of 120 mg remained safe over the entire 24-hour period, and no adjustment was necessary. Students may suggest a variety of advantages for having a dose that remains effective over an entire 24-hour period, including minimizing disruptions in the patient's sleep schedule and daily activities.

4. *a* and *b*. Using the sample data, we find the ratio 63.77/120 ≈ 0.53. So approximately 53 percent of the initial dose of the drug remains in the body after 24 hours, and 47 percent has been eliminated.

5. *a* and *b*. Students' functions and explanations will vary. Working with the sample data, we can determine the following function for the amount of drug in the body at time t: $A = 120(0.90^{t/4})$.

Solutions for "Fine-Tuning a Dosage and a Schedule"

Healthy Dose—Part 2

Students' responses will vary. The table below depicts the level of the drug in the body at the end of every 4–hour interval in a two-day period for a patient receiving a dose of 120 mg once a day.

Time (hr)	Drug Dose (mg)	Amount of Drug in the Body (mg)
0	120	120
4	0	108
8	0	97.2
12	0	87.48
16	0	78.732
20	0	70.8588
24	120	183.77292
28	0	165.39563
32	0	148.85607
36	0	133.97046
40	0	120.57341
44	0	108.51607
48	120	217.66446

1. *a–c*. For the sample dosage of 120 mg in the table, the drug remains safe and effective over a 48-hour period; no adjustment is necessary.

2. *a* and *b*. A patient who takes a 120 mg of the drug once a day, as in the sample data, will have only 53 percent of the dose remaining in his or her body at the end of each 24-hour period. However, with each new dose, the drug level in the body exceeds the level from the same time on the previous day. Nonetheless, with the seventh dose, the level of drug in the patient's body has reached only 253 mg, an amount that is well below the level of toxicity. The students' spreadsheets will look something like that shown in figure 1.7 in the text for 100-mg doses.

3. *a* and *b*. Most students will probably justify their responses with graphs that look something like the sample in figure 1.8 in the text. Students in calculus or precalculus classes may support their answers with arguments based on limits or equilibrium values (see the discussion on pp. 24–25).

Solutions for "Scoping Out the Territory"

Nearest Neighbors–Part 1

1. Students' criteria will vary. It is important to let the students share their ideas and refine their models. They are likely to come up with ideas that are akin to the nearest-neighbor principle.

2. *a* and *b*. Students' responses will vary but should take into account the centers—nests, dens, and so forth—of the territories, as well as the animals' apparent preferences for remaining close to those centers. Students should also consider the regions and boundaries determined by the centers.

3. *a–c*. Students' responses will vary but should apply their developing ideas about centers and the boundaries and regions determined by the nearest-neighbor principle to the three types of decisions: a citizen's decision about which pizzeria in the exclusive chain to patronize, a businessperson's decision about where to open a new pizzeria in the same chain, and a corporate decision by a competing chain about whether or where to build a pizzeria in the city.

4. *a–c*. Students' responses will vary, but they should note that each of the situations in numbers 1–3 has a center of interest—a school, a nest, or a pizzeria. In each case, defining territory involves defining regions around similar centers by apportioning a certain area to each. Students may observe that each region has a boundary that they can determine by a mathematical principle. A point on the boundary must be equidistant from each of the centers on whose boundary it lies. This principle assigns each point in the plane to the center that is closest to it. You may need to help your students refine their descriptions of the common features and principles to include the following information:

   • A boundary line between two centers is the perpendicular bisector of the segment connecting the two centers.
   • Points on the boundary are equidistant from the centers that determine the boundary.
   • A region consists of a center and all the points in the plane that are closer to that center than to any other center.

5. Students' drawings will vary. Some of them are likely to have shapes similar to those shown in the activity's discussion.

6. Students' responses will vary.

Solutions for "Voronoi Vantage Points"

Nearest Neighbors–Part 2

Students' projects will vary according to the situations that they model. Pay careful attention to how the students resolve the mathematical issues that are specific to their situations and apply or modify the nearest-neighbor rule. Check to make sure that the students have completed all the elements outlined in the activity sheet.

Solutions for "Transformers"

1 and 2. The list of points and graph for *P′* under the translation $T(x, y) = (x + 4, y + 3)$ are as follows:

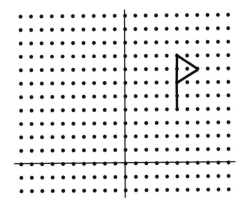

P′	
x	y
5	4
5	8
7	7
5	6

4. The list of points and graph for P' under the transformation $r_{y\text{-axis}}(x, y) = (-x, y)$ follow:

P'	
x	y
−1	1
−1	5
−3	4
−1	3

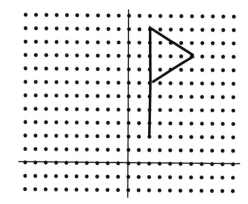

5. The list of points and graph for P' under the dilation $D(x, y) = (2x, 2y)$ follow:

P'	
x	y
2	2
2	10
6	8
2	6

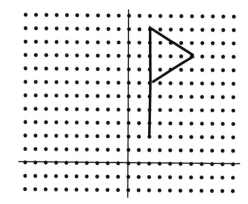

6. The list of points and graph for P' under the two-dimensional scale change $S(x, y) = (0.5x, 2y)$ follow:

P'	
x	y
0.5	2
0.5	10
1.5	8
0.5	6

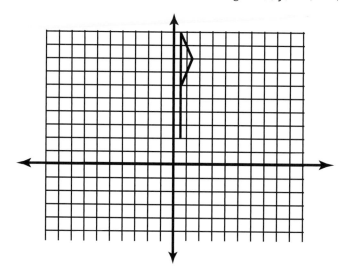

7. a. Area $(P) = 0.5(2)(2) = 2$; area $(P') = 0.5(4)(4) = 8$. Since the dilation doubles distances in the horizontal and vertical directions, the base and height of the original triangular flag are doubled, yielding a triangular flag with four times the original area.

 b. Area $(P) = 0.5(2)(2) = 2$; area $(P') = 0.5[(0.5)(2)][(2)(2)] = 2$. The scale change doubles distances in the vertical direction and halves distances in the horizontal direction. The base of the flag doubles, and its height shrinks to half its original height. Thus, the transformed triangular flag has the same area as the original flag. In general, if a transformation is of the form $M(x, y) = (ax, by)$, then the areas of transformed figures change by a factor of $|ab|$.

8. *a.* A transformation rule that translates P so that the base of the flagpole is at $(-4, 1)$ is $T(x, y) = (x - 5, y - 2)$.

   b. A transformation rule that dilates P so that the area of the flag determined by P' is nine times that of P is $D(x, y) = (3x, 3y)$.

   c. A transformation rule that reflects P about the x-axis is $r(x, y) = (x, -y)$.

   d. A transformation rule that makes the height of the flagpole determined by P' equal to the horizontal width of its flag is $S(x, y) = (2x, y)$.

   e. A transformation rule that transforms P so that P' is upside down, with the base of its flagpole located at $(-4, 6)$ is $F(x, y) = (x - 5, -y + 7)$.

9. Students' answers may vary. Possible observations include the following:

	Properties of the figure that change	Properties of the figure that remain the same
Translation	No fixed points	Lengths of segments and angle measure (shape and size), area, orientation
Reflection	Orientation; only fixed points lie on the line of reflection	Lengths of segments and angle measure (shape and size), area
Dilation	Lengths and area, size	Angle measures, shape, orientation, slopes, ratios of lengths and ratios of area
Scale change	Length, angle measure, size and shape, orientation	Number of sides and vertices, collinearity

Solutions for "The Function of Parents"

1– 2. L is the solid line in the graph, and L' is the dashed line in the graph.

$L: 3x + 4y = 12$	$T(x, y) = (x - 5, y + 2) = (x', y')$	$L': 3x + 4y = 5$

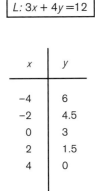

x	y
−4	6
−2	4.5
0	3
2	1.5
4	0

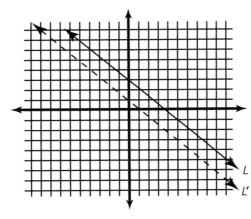

x'	y'
−9	8
−7	6.5
−5	5
−3	3.5
−1	2

3. Substituting $x' + 5$ for x and $y' - 2$ for y in the equation $3x + 4y = 12$ gives a result of $3(x' + 5) + 4(y' - 2) = 12$. Therefore, $3x' + 4y' = 5$. Renaming this equation, we get the equation for L', $3x + 4y = 5$.

4. *a–c.* The equations for L' in numbers 2 and 3 are equivalent. Using the inverse is another way to look at the process. It is an easy way to remember how to generate the equation for the transformed function. In this case, $T(x, y) = (x - 5, y + 2)$. $T^{-1}(x, y)$ is obtained by solving for x and y in terms of x' and y' $(x = x' + 5, y = y' - 2)$. Thus, $(x, y) = T^{-1}(x', y') = (x' + 5, y' - 2)$. Rewriting the rule for $T^{-1}(x', y')$ in standard format gives a result of $T^{-1}(x, y) = (x + 5, y - 2)$. Substituting $x + 5$ for x and $y - 2$ for y in the equation $3x + 4y = 12$ yields the equation $3(x + 5) + 4(y - 2) = 12$, or $3x + 4y = 5$, which is the equation for L'.

5. *a.* The figure at the right shows the graph of *P* and *P'*.

   b. The connection diagram should have the following appearance:

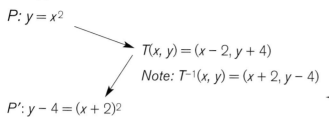

$P: y = x^2$

$T(x, y) = (x - 2, y + 4)$

Note: $T^{-1}(x, y) = (x + 2, y - 4)$

$P': y - 4 = (x + 2)^2$

6. *a.* The connection diagram for the translation $S(x, y) = (6x, 2y)$ follows:

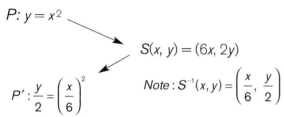

$P: y = x^2$

$S(x, y) = (6x, 2y)$

Note: $S^{-1}(x, y) = \left(\dfrac{x}{6}, \dfrac{y}{2}\right)$

$P': \dfrac{y}{2} = \left(\dfrac{x}{6}\right)^2$

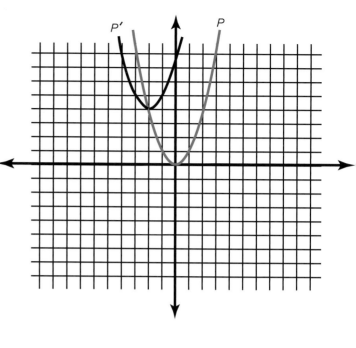

   b. A scale change that maps the point (2, 4) on the graph of $y = x^2$ to the point (6, 2) on the other quadratic is

$$S(x, y) = \left(3x, \frac{1}{2}y\right); \quad P': 2y = \left(\frac{x}{3}\right)^2.$$

The students should find that 6(*a*) and (*b*) both yield the equation $y = x^2/18$. Although the transformations associate the points of *P* and *P'* differently, the two sets of points generated by the transformations are the same.

   c. By choosing any point on *P* other than the vertex, an appropriate scale change on *P* can map that point to the desired location on *P'*.

   d. The image of a parabola under a scale change is always a parabola. Letting $S(x, y) = (rx, sy)$ transforms

$$P: y = ax^2 + bx + c \text{ to } P': \frac{y}{s} = a\left(\frac{x}{r}\right)^2 + b\left(\frac{x}{r}\right) + c, \text{ which is a quadratic function.}$$

7. $S(x, y) = (11x, -8y) \rightarrow P': \dfrac{y}{-8} = \left(\dfrac{x}{11}\right)^2 \rightarrow T(x, y) = (x - 6, y + 7) \rightarrow P'': \dfrac{y - 7}{-8} = \left(\dfrac{x + 6}{11}\right)^2.$

Solutions for "Slinky Transformations"

1. The period is indicated by the distance between the *x*-coordinates of consecutive relative minima on the graph. The relative minima given in the problem indicate that the period is approximately 2.838 − 1.591, or 1.247, seconds.

2. The amplitude is half the distance between the *y*-coordinates of the relative minima and the maxima. The students should use the chart to find the *y*-coordinates of known maxima and minima. Thus, one possible approximation for the amplitude is 0.5(0.793 − 0.120), or 0.337, meters.

3. The period of the cosine function is 2π, and its amplitude is 1.

4. The period of the scatterplot is $\left(\dfrac{1.247}{2\pi} \times \text{period of } \cos x\right) \text{sec}.$

5. The amplitude of the cosine function must be multiplied by 0.337 meters to obtain the amplitude of the scatterplot found in number 2.

6. The following completed connection diagram uses the scale-change transformation suggested by numbers 4 and 5.

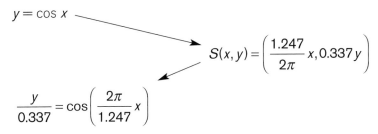

$$y = \cos x$$

$$S(x,y) = \left(\frac{1.247}{2\pi}x, 0.337y\right)$$

$$\frac{y}{0.337} = \cos\left(\frac{2\pi}{1.247}x\right)$$

7. The graph varies in the vertical direction from 0.112 to 0.794. The "midline" of the data set would therefore be the line $y = (0.112 + 0.794)/2$, or $y = 0.453$.

8. A function model for the data set follows:

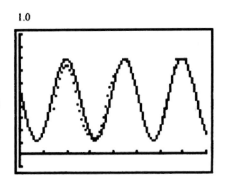

$$\frac{y}{0.337} = \cos\left(\frac{2\pi}{1.247}x\right)$$

$$T(x, y) = (x + 2.236, y + 0.453)$$

$$\frac{y - 0.453}{0.337} = \cos\left(\frac{2\pi}{1.247}(x - 2.236)\right)$$

9. The graph of the function appears at the right. This function graph matches the scatterplot of the data fairly well in the time interval between 2 and 4 seconds. Because the person holding the Slinky spring toy cannot keep the fixed end of the Slinky toy at exactly the same height while its other end oscillates over the sensor, the function can be expected to vary somewhat from the scatterplot for some oscillations, as the graph shows between 0.5 and 2 seconds.

1.0

Solutions for "Sum Squares"

Line 'Em Up–Part 1
1. *a.* The coordinates of the vertex of the graph of the function $y = 5x^2 - 40x + 128$ are (4, 48). The minimum value of y is 48. The graph has no x-intercepts.
   b. The x-coordinate of the vertex is the average of the x-intercepts.
   c. $x_{vertex} = \dfrac{x_1 + x_2}{2} = \dfrac{-b}{2a}$.
   d.

   $$y = ax^2 + bx + c$$

   $$x_{vertex} = -b/2a$$

   $$T(x, y) = (x, y + k)$$

   $$y = ax^2 + bx + c + k$$

   e. If the quadratic $y = ax^2 + bx + c$ is translated vertically so that it has two x-intercepts, the resulting quadratic function is $y - k = ax^2 + bx + c$, or $y = ax^2 + bx + c + k$. Students should draw the general conclusion that the x-coordinate of the vertex does not change with vertical translations of the parabola. Thus, for any quadratic of the form $y = ax^2 + bx + c$, the x-coordinate of the vertex is $-b/2a$.

2. *a.* The completed chart follows.

x	y	$Y = mx$	$(y - Y)^2$
−5	−1	−5m	$1 - 10m + 25m^2$
−2	−3	−2m	$9 - 12m + 4m^2$
3	0	3m	$9m^2$
4	4	4m	$16 - 32m + 16m^2$

b. The sum of the squares of the residuals is $54m^2 - 54m + 26$, which is at its minimum when $m = 0.5$.

c. The line of best fit is $Y = 0.5x$.

Solutions for "Find the Line"

Line 'Em Up–Part 2

1. Students' answers will vary. The following response is just one example.

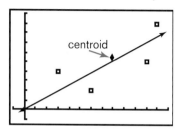

x	y	$Y = 0.6x$	$(y - Y)^2$
3	4	1.8	4.84
6	2	3.6	2.56
11	5	6.6	2.56
12	9	7.2	3.24

Equation of line: $Y = 0.6x$

Sum of squares of residuals: 13.2

2. The centroid is (8, 5) and is indicated (♦) in the scatterplot in number 1.

3. The centroid is very close to the line in the example. Most students should be able to obtain that result.

4 and 5. The following chart continues the example from numbers 1–3, with additional columns to illustrate the computation in number 5.

x	y	$Y = 0.6x - 0.2$	$(y - Y)^2$
−5	−1	−3.2	4.84
−2	−3	−1.4	2.56
3	0	1.6	2.56
4	4	2.2	3.24

The line:

$Y = 0.6x$

$T: (x, y) = (x - \bar{x}, y - \bar{y}) = x - 8, y - 5$

Equation of image:

$Y + 5 = 0.6(x + 8)$

The sum of the squares of the residuals, 13.2, is the same as it was before the transformation. It is important for students to compare their results here. No matter what line they guessed in number 1, the sum of the squares of the residuals does not change under the translation.

6. Students should give an explanation similar to the following: "Translations preserve distances between points. Thus, the sum of the squares of the distances does not change."

7. Students should give an explanation similar to the following: "If L is the line of best fit for a data set D and if the sum of the squares of the residuals is M, then the sum of the squares of the residuals for L', the image of L, and for D', the image of D, is also M. If a line K existed and the sum of the squares of its residuals with respect to D' was $N < M$, then its image under the inverse of the translation would be a line whose sum of squares of residuals with respect to D was N. This result would contradict the fact that M is the smallest sum of squares of residuals for lines with respect to data set D. Thus, L' is the best-fit line for data set D'."

8. Students should provide an explanation similar to the following, which uses ideas from number 7 as its basis: "Since the line of best fit L passes through the centroid $(\bar{x}, \bar{y})$, the image of L under a translation will contain the image of $(\bar{x}, \bar{y})$, which in this case is $(0, 0)$. It is also true that the centroid $(\bar{x}, \bar{y})$ of a data set D is mapped to the centroid of the transformed data set D' under a translation."

9 and 10. Since students must perform the inverse of the translation in number 4, they discover that $T^{-1}(x, y) = (x + 8, y + 5)$. This inverse transforms the line of best fit, $y = 0.5x$, in number 2 in "Sum Squares" to the line $y = 0.5x + 1$. Thus, $y = 0.5x + 1$ is the line of best fit for the data set in number 1 of "Find the Line." This line is the same as the line that the students obtain by using the linear regression option on the calculator.

11. Students should describe the following process to find the line of best fit:

a. Find the mean of the x-values and the mean of the y-values of the data set. In this example, $\bar{x} = 1$ and $\bar{y} = 4$, so the centroid of the data set is $(1, 4)$.

b. Translate the data set so that the point $(1, 4)$ is moved to the origin. In this example, the translation is $T(x, y) = (x - 1, y - 4)$, and the transformed data set is $\{(1, -1), (-4, 1), (3, 0)\}$.

c. For the transformed data set, find the line through the origin whose sum of squares of residuals is the minimum. In this example, the equation of the best-fit line is $y = \dfrac{-5}{26}x$.

d. Find the image of $y = \dfrac{-5}{26}x$ under the inverse of the translation: $T^{-1}(x, y) = (x + 1, y + 4)$. In this example, the image is

$$\left(y - 4\right) = \frac{-5}{26}(x - 1), \text{ or } y = \frac{-5}{26}x + 4\frac{5}{26}.$$

Note: Students should understand that they do not need transformations to find the line of best fit for a data set. Armed only with the knowledge that the vertex of the quadratic function $f(x) = ax^2 + bx + c$ occurs at $x = -b/2a$, they can directly prove that the centroid is on the line of best fit, and they can use that information to find the line of best fit.

For the proof, the students can consider the family of parallel lines with a fixed slope m. Each of these lines intersects the vertical line $x = \bar{x}$ at some point $(\bar{x}, h)$. To find the h that minimizes the sum of the squares of the residuals, they can use the data set to find the sum of the squares of the residuals of the line $y = m(x - \bar{x}) + h$. The resulting expression will be a quadratic in the variable h whose minimum they can establish by applying the fact that for the quadratic function $f(x) = ax^2 + bx + c$, the vertex occurs at $x = -b/2a$. Thus, the minimum occurs when $h = \bar{y}$.

Next, to find the line of best fit, the students can consider the set of all nonvertical lines that pass through the centroid. These lines all have equations of the form $y = m(x - \bar{x}) + \bar{y}$. To find the m that minimizes the sum of the squares of the residuals, they can use the data set to find the sum of the squares of the residuals of the line $y = m(x - \bar{x}) + \bar{y}$. The resulting expression is a quadratic in the variable m whose minimum they can establish by using $x = -b/2a$ again. By finding m and knowing that the line of best fit passes through $(\bar{x}, \bar{y})$, they can determine the line of best fit.

Solutions for "Tiles in a Row"

1. The following diagram shows a row in which colored tiles surround 4 white square tiles.

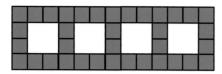

The following diagram shows a row in which colored tiles surround 5 white squares.

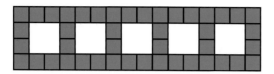

2. Students may use different methods to determine the number of colored tiles that are in a row without actually counting them all. Two examples follow:

   a. Some students might count the 8 colored tiles on the top, the left side, and the bottom of each white square tile, multiply 8 times the number of white square tiles, and add the 4 colored tiles on the right end, finding that $(8 \times 5) + 4 = 44$, the number of colored tiles surrounding 5 white tiles.

   b. Some students might draw the diagram with 5 white squares enclosed by colored tiles and decide to use the length of a colored tile as the unit length. Thus, the diagram would appear to be a rectangle with a length of 16 units and a width of 4 units. Since the area of the rectangle is 64 square units and the area of the 5 enclosed white tiles is $5 \times (2 \times 2)$, or 20, square units, the area corresponding to the colored tiles is $64 - 20$, or 44, square units. Thus, the students would need 44 colored tiles.

3. Students' methods may vary, but they should determine that they need 52 colored tiles for a row that has 6 white square tiles.

4. Students' methods may vary, but they should determine that they need 84 colored tiles for a row with 10 white square tiles. Students might count the 8 colored tiles on the top, the left side, and the bottom of each white square, multiply 8 times the number of white squares to obtain a result of 80, and then add the 4 colored tiles on the right end to determine that 84 colored tiles are ncessary.

5. Using the method employed in the solution to number 4, students multiply 8 times the number of white square tiles, N, to obtain $8N$. They then add the 4 colored tiles on the end to obtain a result of $8N + 4$.

6. If a row takes 116 colored tiles for a complete pattern, then the row includes 14 white tiles:

$$8N + 4 = 116$$
$$8N = 11$$
$$N = 14$$

Solutions for "Constructing a Tape"

Measurement in the Round–Part 1

2. The students' methods for finding the center of the circle will vary. Students can fold their circles in half along two different lines. The point at which the fold lines intersect is the center. Another method is to use a straightedge to draw two nonparallel chords and find the intersection of the perpendicular bisectors of those two chords. Some students might suggest using a Mira to find the center of the circle.

3. Students' explanations may vary. One possible explanation follows: "The center of a circle is equidistant from every point on the circle. Furthermore, any point that is equidistant from the endpoints of a segment must lie on the perpendicular bisector of that segment. The center of the circle must therefore lie on the perpendicular bisector of all

its chords. Only one such point exists, and it can be found by locating the intersection of the perpendicular bisectors of two nonparallel chords."

6. Students can use various strategies to mark and label points without using a ruler. For example, by lightly folding their strips of paper so that the mark for a number N lies on the mark for the number $N + 1$, the students can find the location for $N + 1/2$.

7. Students should obtain a number that is close to 6. Sometimes the rim of the can that determines the unit circle is slightly larger than the surface of the can. This rim typically adds nearly an eighth of an inch to the circumference. Therefore, students might obtain more accurate results if they wrap their tape around the rim of the can instead of the center. If your students do not recognize that the number is an approximation of 2π, you should review the formula that gives the relationship between the circumference of a circle and its radius—that is, $C = 2\pi \cdot r$.

8. The students' work should show them that π is half the circumference.

9. One of the compass-and-straightedge constructions that students learn in high school geometry is to divide a segment into a given number of equal parts. The construction requires drawing a set of equally spaced parallel lines. Notebook paper can provide a suitable set of equally spaced parallel lines, and the following diagram illustrates how to divide a segment into five equal parts. Placing the segment so that it exactly spans six of the parallel lines (and consequently the five equal gaps between them) partitions the segment into five equal parts at the points where the parallel lines intersect the segment.

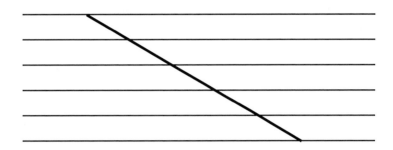

Solutions for "Measuring Angles"

Measurement in the Round—Part 2

2. Students' answers will vary.

3. *a–d.* The radian measure of the directed angle whose arc of rotation corresponds to the upper half of the unit circle is π, and the radian measure of the angle whose arc of rotation corresponds to the fourth of the unit circle that is contained in the first quadrant is $\pi/2$. These arcs are, respectively, one-half and one-fourth of the entire circumference, which is 2π, the solution in 3(*c*).

4. The following graphs show the directed angles that students obtain.

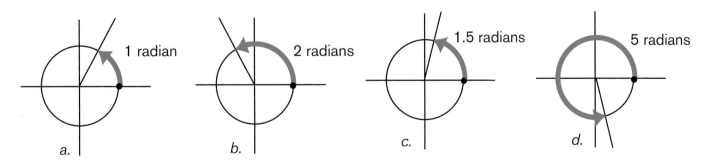

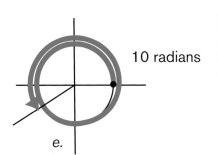

10 radians

In 4(e), students need to recognize that the arc of rotation can exceed one complete revolution around the vertex. Even though the arc of rotation is measured strictly along the unit circle, the drawing shows that the arc of rotation exceeds one complete revolution around the vertex.

e.

5. In explaining why angles for a particular number of radians constructed by two students who used different-sized cans appear to be congruent, students often use proportional reasoning. When the radius of one circle is greater than the radius of the other circle, the arc in the larger circle is proportionately longer than the corresponding arc in the smaller circle.

6. a. The associated angles are $\dfrac{\pi}{2}, \dfrac{5\pi}{2}, \dfrac{9\pi}{2}, \ldots,$ and $\dfrac{-3\pi}{2}, \dfrac{-7\pi}{2}, \dfrac{-11\pi}{2}, \ldots.$

   b. Negative radian measures correspond to directed angles that represent rotations in the clockwise direction. Positive radian measures correspond to directed angles that represent rotations in the counterclockwise direction.

Solutions for "Graphing Circular Functions"

Measurement in the Round—Part 3

1. The following graph shows the sine function between −4 and 4.

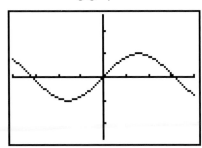

2. The following graph shows the cosine function between −4 and 4.

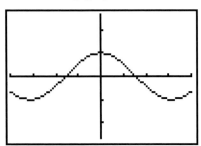

3. The graph at the right shows the tangent function between −4 and 4.

   The graph of the tangent function between −4 and 4 has vertical asymptotes at $\dfrac{\pm\pi}{2}$.

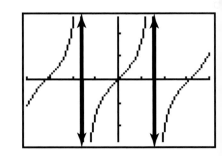

4. The graph of the tangent function is not defined at the vertical asymptotes. The behavior is shown in the solution to number 3.

5. The students should notice that the functions are periodic, and some will note that the graphs repeat at intervals of 2π. The tangent graph repeats at intervals of π. The students' graphs should have essentially the same shape and behaviors, differing only in their relative sizes.

Solution for "Interpreting Transit Graphs"

Assuming $T = 0$ at midnight, observers at the 10-km mark would see (1) five southbound ships at 15-minute intervals, beginning at $T = 4$, or 4:00 a.m. (that is, at 4:00, 4:15, 4:30, 4:45, and 5:00 a.m.); (2) one northbound ship at $T \approx 8.5$, or approximately 8:30 a.m.; (3) that same ship, now southbound, at $T \approx 14.5$, or approximately 2:30 p.m.; (4) five more southbound ships at 15-minute intervals, beginning at $T = 16$, or 4:00 p.m. (that is, at 4:00, 4:15, 4:30, 4:45, and 5:00 p.m.); and (5) one northbound ship at $T \approx 20$, or approximately 9:00 p.m.

Solutions for "Graphs That Tell Stories"

Transit Graphs–Part 1

1. The students' answers will vary. A ship departed from the south end of the canal at the 0-hour mark. It traveled at a speed of 5 km/hr for 6 hours and then stopped at the 30-kilometer mark for 8 hours. It finally completed its journey to the north end of the canal, traveling at a speed of 2.5 km/hr. One possible explanation for the shape of the graph is that the ship developed engine trouble at the 30-kilometer mark and that after the repairs were completed, it was unable to travel as fast as it had previously traveled. Another explanation might be that the ship took on a load of cargo in an unlabeled bypass zone and had to proceed more slowly because of its additional weight.

2. The graph depicts the movements of two ships. One ship left the south end of the canal at the 0-hour mark. It traveled at a speed of 5 km/hr for 6 hours and then came to a stop at the 6-hour mark, remaining at rest until the 8-hour mark, a period of 2 hours. (Perhaps it unloaded cargo there in an unlabeled bypass zone.) The ship then reversed its direction and traveled at a speed of 7.5 km/hr back to the south end of the canal. It had barely exited the canal when a faster-moving southbound ship arrived from the north. This second ship began its uninterrupted journey south through the canal at the 8-hour mark and completed its transit of the canal in 4 hours, traveling at a rate of 12.5 km/hr.

3. The graph depicts three northbound ships departing at the 0-hour, 12-hour, and 18-hour marks. These ships traveled at 50/18 = 2.78 km/hr, 50/7 = 7.14 km/hr, and 50/2 = 25 km/hr, respectively.

4. The graph depicts the transit of two convoys of closely spaced ships. The first ship of the northbound convoy departed at the 0-hour mark; and the ninth ship, the last one in the convoy, departed at the 4-hour mark. The nine ships departed at 30-minute intervals and began arriving at the north end of the canal at the 5-hour mark, with ships arriving every 30 minutes until the last ship arrived at the 9-hour mark. All the ships traveled at a rate of 10 km/hr. The southbound convoy is a mirror image of the first convoy. The nine ships traveled at a rate of 10 km/hr, with 30 minutes separating ships. The first ship of that convoy departed from the north end of the canal at the 12-hour mark and arrived at the south end of the canal at the 17-hour mark. The last ship departed from the north end of the canal at the 16-hour mark and arrived at the south end of the canal at the 21-hour mark.

5. *a.*

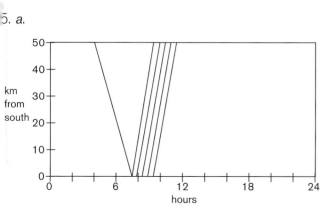

b.

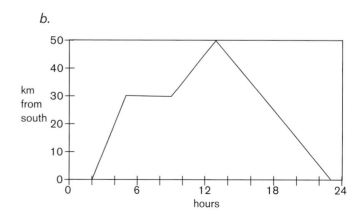

Solutions for "Creating Optimal Schedules"

Transit Graphs—Part 2

1. The optimal schedule at the right shows the first north-bound ship entering the canal at the 0-hour mark and the last southbound ship leaving the canal at the 24-hour mark.

   The northbound ships have a 12-hour block (between the 0-hour and 12-hour marks on the graph) to complete their trips, and the southbound ships have a 12-hour block (between the 12-hour and 24-hour marks on the graph). Since a ship takes 5 hours to pass through the canal, all the northbound ships must arrive at the north end of the canal between hour marks 5 and

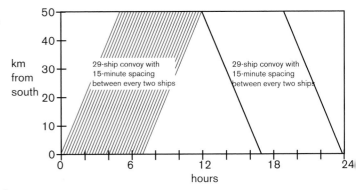

   12 on the graph. A total of 29 ships can travel 15 minutes apart in a 7-hour time block. When many ships travel in a continuous convoy, transit graphs often show only the first and last ships, as the graph does with the southbound convoy.

2. Reasoning similar to that used in number 1 applies to this problem. The following graph illustrates the solution.

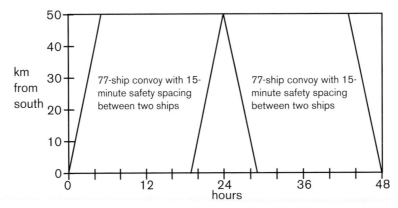

3. The efficiency of the 48-hour cycle is greater than that of the 24-hour cycle because a smaller relative percentage of the available time is spent waiting for the last ship in each convoy to move out of the way. A total of 58 ships, or 2.4 ships each hour, can pass through the canal in the 24-hour cycle. A total of 154 ships, or 3.2 ships per hour, can pass through the canal in the 48-hour cycle.

4. Students should consider two cycles in their graphs—one for the northbound ships (shown in purple in the graph below) and one for the southbound ships (shown in gray).

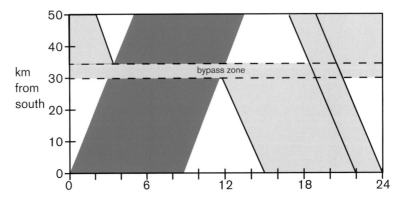

The northbound ships (purple) must pass through the canal without stopping. The optimal graph schedules all the northbound ships to enter the canal between the 0-hour mark and the 9-hour mark, and it schedules them to leave the canal between the 5-hour mark and the 14-hour mark. The total number of these northbound ships is 37

Passage through the canal on the optimal schedule is more complicated for the southbound ships (gray). Most of these ships must stop and dock in the bypass zone while northbound ships pass. The optimal schedule allows only 9 southbound ships—those that enter the canal between the 17-hour mark and the 19-hour mark—to pass through without stopping. (Note that the graph marks these ships off from the other southbound ships by line segments for ease of interpretation.) Nevertheless, the graph shows 28 additional southbound ships entering the canal at the north end and 28 leaving the canal at the south end, for a total of 37 southbound ships entering and leaving the canal in a 24-hour period. Students should note that the graph shows equal areas of purple and gray (outside the bypass zone), representing equal numbers of northbound and southbound ships. However, of the 37 total ships that the graph shows leaving the canal at the south end, 19 entered the canal between 19.25 and 24 hours on the *previous* day, and the 19 ships that the graph shows entering the canal between the 19.25-hour and 24-hour marks will finish their journeys on the *next* day, starting at the 12-hour mark, after stopping in the bypass zone. As the text explains, these two incomplete bands of ships represent a single complete band in the graph of a repeating schedule.

Solutions for "Selecting a Location"

Quick Response Time—Part 1

1. The average response time is shortest when the average distance to the towns is least. But the average is the sum of the distances to the towns divided by 3, so it will be smallest when the sum of the three distances is the smallest. One assumption in this explanation is that the traffic flow on the highway is uniform.

2. *a.* If the planners decide to locate the fire station at milepost 13, it will be 8 miles from Littleton, 4 miles from Smallsville, and 7 miles from Tinytown.

   b. The total distance from the fire station to the three towns will be 19 miles.

3. The total distance will be 15.5 miles.

4. *a.* The "best" location for the fire station, in the sense of minimizing the total distance to the three towns, is milepost 17.

   b. Students will give various justifications for their solutions. Students may make a chart similar to the following one and may base their justifications on the pattern that they observe in the distances:

Milepost	14	15	16	17	18	19	20
Total distance	18	17	16	15	16	17	18

   Students must understand that such a chart does not prove that the minimum occurs at milepost 17, because it does not indicate the distances for locations between mileposts.

   Some students may argue correctly that since any point between Littleton and Smallsville yields the same total distance from the station to the two towns (12 miles), picking the point in the interval from milepost 12 to milepost 17 that is closest to Tinytown will minimize the total distance. Therefore, milepost 17 is the optimal location between mileposts 12 and 17. Students can apply the same argument to the set of points in the interval from milepost 20 to milepost 17. Thus, milepost 17 is the optimal location.

5. If the three towns are at mileposts 55, 59, and 70, the best location appears to be milepost 59. For any three towns on the highway, the location that minimizes the total distance to the three towns is the middle town, which is therefore the best location for the fire station.

6. *a.* If the four towns are at mileposts 0, 5, 17, and 20, any location for the fire station between or at mileposts 5 and 17 will minimize the distances.

   b. Students' ideas may vary about whether the procedure that they outlined for the solution in number 5 applies to the four-town scenario.

7. *a.* The students' procedures for locating the station may vary. When the number of towns is even, students must locate the fire station between the middle two towns or at one of them.

   b. The students' examples will vary.

8. *a–c.* If Bug Crossing and Punyberg join Littleton, Smallsville, and Tinytown in building the fire station, the five towns should locate the station at milepost 17, which is the middle number of the towns' milepost numbers. Some students will notice that the best location is always the middle milepost number when the number of towns is odd. Some students will realize that the best locations occur at the middle pair of milepost numbers and at any point between them when the number of towns is even. Therefore, to minimize the total of the distances to the towns, locating the station at the median of the data set is sufficient.

Students might consider additional examples to make their point. Some might carry their thinking even further, reasoning that when the number of towns is odd and *D* is the total of the distances with the station at the median *M,* moving the station even one mile to the west of *M* increases the distances for more than half the towns (those to the east of *M,* as well as the town at *M*) by one mile and decreases the distances of fewer than half of the towns by at most a mile. The result is that the total distance increases by at least one mile. The students can apply the same argument to moving the station even one mile to the east of *M.*

9. *a.* One argument that students should raise is that the response time for both Bug Crossing and Littleton is significantly worse than the response time for the other towns. The plan in number 8 favors the towns in the east.

   b. These towns might argue that a better location would be at the midpoint between Bug Crossing and Punyberg.

Solutions for "Generalizing Results"

Quick Response Time–Part 2

1. Students should use absolute values to write expressions for the distances to each of the towns from *x,* the location of the fire station. The distance to Littleton is $|x - 5|$, the distance to Smallsville is $|x - 17|$, and the distance to Tinytown is $|x - 20|$.

2. A function that gives the total distance from the fire station to the original three towns in terms of *x,* the location of the fire station, is $f(x) = |x - 5| + |x - 17| + |x - 20|$.

3. *a and b.* Figure 4.1 (p. 68) shows a graph of the function. The graph does seem to confirm that milepost 17, the location that students should have determined in number 4 of "Selecting a Location," is optimal. However, although the graph is visually compelling, it is not a proof. It is impossible to observe every possible value of *x* near 17 to verify that 17 gives the minimum total distance.

4. From a statistical point of view, the best location of the fire station for the original three towns is the median of the set {5, 17, 20}.

5. The modified function that incorporates Bug Crossing, at milepost 0, is

$$f(x) = |x - 0| + |x - 5| + |x - 17| + |x - 20|.$$

The students' graphs should support their solutions. Figure 4.2 (p. 68) shows a graph of the function.

6. The modified function that incorporates Punyberg, at milepost 23, is

$$f(x) = |x - 0| + |x - 5| + |x - 17| + |x - 20| + |x - 23|.$$

The students' graphs should support their solutions. Figure 4.3 (p. 69) shows a graph of the function.

7. Students should conclude that if the towns locate the fire station at the median of the town mileposts, they will minimize the total distance.

Solutions for "The Fairest of Them All"

Quick Response Time–Part 3

1. *a.* The location that is exactly halfway between Bug Crossing and Punyberg is at milepost 11.5. The total distance to the five towns is 43.5 miles.

   b. Of all the potential centers, this location is about as close to Bug Crossing as the residents of Bug Crossing can realistically hope that the other towns will consider. The plan is reasonable, and the other towns might go along with it. However, residents of other towns might believe that the plan favors the towns on the west, since the total of the distances to towns on the west of this milepost is 18 miles, and the total of the distances to the towns on the east is 25.5 miles.

2. *a* and *b*. The point on the highway from which the total distances to the cities on the west equals the total distances to the cities on the east is at milepost 13. A quick way to find this point is to average, or find the mean of, the mileposts for the towns. The total distance from this milepost to all the towns is 42 miles. By comparison, if the station were located at the median, or milepost 17, the total distance would be 37 miles.

3. *a*. If a town is west of *x*, then the difference between *x* and that town's milepost is positive. If a town is east of *x*, then the difference between *x* and that town's milepost is negative. Therefore, when the distances to the east exactly balance with the distances to the west, the sum of those positive and negative differences is 0.

   b. The equation $(x - 0) + (x - 5) + (x - 17) + (x - 20) + (x - 23) = 0$ generalizes to the following:

   $$(x - a) + (x - b) + (x - c) + (x - d) + (x - e) = 0.$$

   Combining like terms gives $5x - (a + b + c + d + e) = 0$. Thus, *x* is equal to the mean, since

   $$x = \frac{a+b+c+d+e}{5}.$$

4. *a*. Students' answers will vary, depending on the locations that they have selected for the fire station.

   b. Smallsville, at milepost 17, is not the best location for the fire station if the goal is to minimize the sum of the squares of the distances. Using that criterion, students may find several mileposts that are better.

   c. If the goal is to minimize the sum of the squares of the distances, the best location is milepost 13, the mean. Students might make a chart or use a function and a graph to find this solution. On the basis of the students' work in "Selecting a Location" and "Generalizing Results," both strategies can emerge. Students who use a graph will obtain the following function: $f(x) = (x - 0)^2 + (x - 5)^2 + (x - 17)^2 + (x - 20)^2 + (x - 23)^2$. Thus, $f(x) = 5x^2 - 2(0 + 5 + 17 + 20 + 23)x + (0^2 + 5^2 + 17^2 + 20^2 + 23^2)$, or $f(x) = 5x^2 - 130x + 1243$. This equation is a quadratic with minimum at

   $$x = \frac{-b}{2a} = \frac{130}{2(5)} = 13.$$

5. Expressions for the squared distance from each of the towns to the fire station located at point *x* are as follows:

Town	Distance to Fire Station
Bug Crossing	$(x - 0)^2$
Littleton	$(x - 5)^2$
Smallsville	$(x - 17)^2$
Tinytown	$(x - 20)^2$
Punyberg	$(x - 23)^2$

   a. A function that gives the total of the squared distances from the five towns to the fire station in terms of *x*, the milepost of the fire station is $f(x) = (x - 0)^2 + (x - 5)^2 + (x - 17)^2 + (x - 20)^2 + (x - 23)^2$.

   . The graph of the function is a parabola with minimum at (13, 229). It does not favor towns on the east or west. It does not minimize the total of the distances to the towns; however, from the point of view of service, it is fairer to the towns of Bug Crossing and Littleton than a location at the median. It might have the best chance of satisfying political considerations and being adopted.

Solutions for "Double-Dare Simulation"

le-Dare—Part 2

ents' answers will vary.

lents' results will vary.

students play 30 games and use the "I quit" strategy each time, they should expect to lose 30 points.

though the "play-on" strategy should give students a better score, students' answers may vary.

ions

4. *a.* The expected value of the "I quit" strategy is −1 point.

   b. Students' answers will vary, depending on the results of their simulations.

   c. The number that is larger is the expected value that is better for the student.

Solutions for "Double-Dare Theory"

Double-Dare—Part 3

1. If a person uses the "I quit" strategy in 30 games, his or her expected value is −1 point. Since he or she loses one point for each game, the total is −30, and the average per game is −30/30, or −1.

2. *a.* Students should expect to win 10 games and lose 20. Therefore, they should expect to win 20 points and lose 40 points, for a point total of −20. Since they play 30 games, the average score is −20/30, or −2/3.

   b. Students' answers will vary depending on the estimate that they made from their simulations.

3. Students should recognize that the "play on" strategy is better in the long run, since it results in an expected average loss of 2/3 point each game.

4. *a.* If someone uses the "play on" strategy in 75 games, he or she should expect to lose 50 games and win 25 games. Therefore, this player should expect to lose 100 points and win 50 points, for a point total of −50. The average score per game is −50/75. That is, students should expect to lose an average of 2/3 point per game.

   b. The number of games does not affect this theoretical calculation. For 75 games, the average number of points won or lost per game is $\dfrac{2 \times 25 - 2 \times 50}{75}$.

   By replacing the 25 and 50 by the operation that generated them, students obtain a result of

   $$\frac{2 \times \left(\dfrac{1}{3} \times 75\right) - 2 \times \left(\dfrac{2}{3} \times 75\right)}{75}.$$

   By factoring out the 75s and simplifying, they get $2 \times \dfrac{1}{3} - 2 \times \dfrac{2}{3}$.

   Students should notice that the choice of 75 games does not influence the outcome. With any number of games, the expected value is $2 \times \dfrac{1}{3} - 2 \times \dfrac{2}{3}$.

5. Students' answers will vary, depending on the probabilities of losing that they select.

6. No matter what the probability of losing is, the expected value for the "I quit" strategy is always −1.

7. As the probability of losing increases, the expected value for the "play on" strategy approaches −2 because a player loses more often and wins less often. When the probability of losing reaches 1, the expected value for the "play on" strategy reaches the limit of −2.

8. Students' answers will vary. Students who investigate the expected values when the probability of losing is three fourths will find that the expected values for both strategies are −1. They are in a position to draw the correct conclusion that the "play on" strategy is better than the "I quit" strategy when the probability of losing is less than three-fourths and that the "I quit" strategy is better when the probability of losing is greater than three-fourths.

Solutions for "Double-Dare with Algebra"

Double-Dare—Part 4

1. The expected value for the "I quit" strategy is always −1. The expected value for the "play on" strategy decreases as the probability of losing increases. If the probability of winning is 1 (that is, if the player is certain to win), the expected value of the "play on" strategy is 2; and if the probability of losing is 1 (that is, if the player is certain to lose), the expected value of the "play on" strategy is −2. Somewhere in between, the expected value of the "play on" strategy is −1. As long as the expected value is greater than −1, the "play on" strategy is better than the "I quit" strategy.

2. *a.* If the probability of losing a game is P, the probability of winning the game is $(1 - P)$.

   b. The students should expect to win $100(1 - P)$ games if they use the "play on" strategy for 100 games with a probability P of losing.

   c. The wins in 2(*b*) give $200(1 - P)$ points.

   d. The students should expect to lose $100P$ games.

   e. The students should expect to lose $200P$ points for the games in 2(*d*).

   f. Combining expected wins and losses gives a total expected score of $200(1 - P) - 200P$ for 100 games with the "play on" strategy.

   g. The students should expect a total score of -100 for 100 games with the "I quit" strategy.

3. The equation that indicates when the expected score for the "play on" strategy equals the expected score for the "I quit" strategy is $200(1 - P) - 200P = -100$. Its solution is $P = .75$.

4. A complete plan for deciding when to quit and when to accept a double in a double-dare situation follows: If the probability of losing is less than .75, the player should play on. If the probability of losing is greater than .75, the player should quit. If the probability of losing is equal to .75, the strategy does not matter, since the expected values are the same.

Solutions for "Measuring the Middle Pole"

Support Cables–Part 1

1. Students' answers will vary depending on the scale that they select for the drawing. In the example, in the solutions to steps 2 and 3, the scale of the drawing is 1 unit = 2 feet.

2 and 3. The graph on the left represents the situation in number 2, and the graph on the right represents that in number 3 for a new value of 30 feet for *d*. The height of the middle pole in both instances is $13\frac{1}{3}$ feet (though students may approximate the measure at this stage).

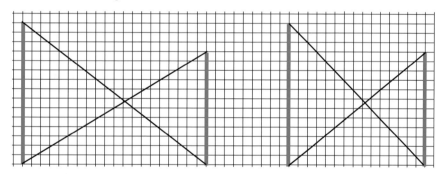

All students should find that their approximations of the height of the middle pole are close to the same number. The height does not depend on the length of the base.

Solutions for "Interactive Measurement"

Support Cables–Part 2

This exploration uses the applet Support Cables, which is available on the CD-ROM accompanying the book. The heights for several selected distances appear below:

d (ft.)	*h* (ft.)
10	13.33
20	13.33
30	13.33
40	13.33
50	13.33

The students should find that the height, h, of the middle pole does not depend on d. Regardless of the distance d, the height is 13.33 feet.

Solutions for "Proving Your Conjecture"

Support Cables–Part 3

1. The similar triangles in the figure are $\triangle ABC$ and $\triangle EDC$, $\triangle ABE$ and $\triangle CFE$, and $\triangle DEB$ and $\triangle CFB$.

2. Since $\overline{AB} \| \overline{DE}$, the students know that $\angle ABD \cong \angle EDB$. Also, $\angle ACB \cong \angle ECD$, since they are vertical angles. The triangles are therefore similar by the angle-angle criterion. The following ratios are equal:

$$\frac{u}{z} = \frac{w}{v} = \frac{30}{24}.$$

3. Since $\overline{AB} \| \overline{CF}$, the students know that $\frac{u}{z} = \frac{x}{y}$. Therefore, $\frac{x}{y} = \frac{30}{24}$. Other proportions are possible, but they yield the same value for h.

4. From number 3, the students know that $x = \frac{30y}{24} = 1.25y$. Since $\triangle ABE \sim \triangle CFE$, they know that $\frac{30}{h} = \frac{x+y}{y}$.

   Thus, $\frac{30}{h} = \frac{1.25y + y}{y} = 2.25$. Therefore, $h = 13\frac{1}{3}$ feet. The solution does not depend on the values of x or y, so it does not depend on the distance between the end poles.

5. The coordinates of D are $(d, 24)$, and the coordinates of E are $(d, 0)$.

6. The equation of the line containing points B and D is $y = \frac{24}{d}x$. The equation of the line containing points A and E is $y = \frac{-30}{d}x + 30$.

7. By setting the equations equal to each other, the students see that $\frac{24}{d}x = \frac{-30}{d}x + 30$. Multiplying each side of the equation by d yields $24x = -30x + 30d$. Therefore, $54x = 30d$, and $x = \frac{30}{54}d = \frac{5}{9}d$. Substituting the x-coordinate into the equation $y = \frac{24}{d}x$ yields a result of $y = \frac{24}{d} \cdot \frac{5}{9}d = \frac{120}{9} = 13\frac{1}{3}$.

8. The y-coordinate of point C does not depend on the length of $\overline{BE}$. However, the x-coordinate does depend on the length of $\overline{BE}$.

Solutions for "Is There a Better Way?"

Support Cables–Part 4

1. $\overline{AB}$ corresponds to $\overline{ED}$, $\overline{CR}$ corresponds to $\overline{CS}$, $\overline{BR}$ corresponds to $\overline{DS}$, $\overline{AR}$ corresponds to $\overline{ES}$, $\overline{AC}$ corresponds to $\overline{EC}$, and $\overline{BC}$ corresponds to $\overline{DC}$.

2. All the ratios are the same and therefore equal 30/24, or 5/4. An alternative solution is of course 24/30, or 4?

3. A proportion that involves only one variable, h, is $\frac{BR}{DS} = \frac{30}{24}$. Therefore, $\frac{h}{24-h} = \frac{30}{24}$, which yields $54h = 720$, or $h = 13\frac{1}{3}$.

4. Since $\frac{BR}{DS} = \frac{p}{q}$, students find that $\frac{h}{q-h} = \frac{p}{q}$, which yields $(p+q)h = pq$, or $h = \frac{pq}{p+q}$.

References

Acker, Kathleen A. "Drug Levels and Difference Equations." *Mathematics Teacher* 98 (November 2004): 266–73.

Boyer, Carl. *A History of Mathematics.* New York: John Wiley & Sons, 1968.

Burke, Maurice J., Paul E. Kehle, Paul A. Kennedy, and Dennis St. John. *Navigating through Number and Operations in Grades 9–12. Principles and Standards for School Mathematics* Navigations Series. Reston, Va.: National Council of Teachers of Mathematics, 2006.

Coffey, Margaret. "Irrational Numbers on the Number Line: Perfectly Placed." *Mathematics Teacher* 94 (September 2001): 453–55.

Cuoco, Al. "Match Making: Fitting Polynomials to Tables." *Mathematics Teacher* 96 (March 2003): 178–83.

Day, Roger, Paul Kelley, Libby Krussel, Johnny W. Lott, and James Hirstein. *Navigating through Geometry in Grades 9–12. Principles and Standards for School Mathematics* Navigations Series. Reston, Va.: National Council of Teachers of Mathematics, 2001.

Dossey, John, Sharon McCrone, Frank Giordana, and Maurice Weir. *Mathematics Methods and Modeling for Today's Classroom: A Contemporary Approach to Teaching Grades 7–12.* Pacific Grove, Calif.: Brooks/Cole Publishing, 2002.

Edwards, Dilwyn, and Mike Hamson. *Guide to Mathematical Modelling.* Boca Raton, Fla.: CRC Press, 1990.

Friel, Susan, Sid Rachlin, and Dot Doyle. *Navigating through Algebra in Grades 6–8. Principles and Standards for School Mathematics* Navigations Series. Reston, Va.: National Council of Teachers of Mathematics, 2001.

Griffiths, J. D., and E. M. Hassan. "Increasing the Shipping Capacity of the Suez Canal." *Journal of Navigation* 31 (May 1978): 218–31.

House, Peggy. "Integrated Mathematics: An Introduction." In *Integrated Mathematics: Choices and Challenges,* edited by Sue Ann McGraw, pp. 3–11. Reston, Va.: National Council of Teachers of Mathematics, 2003.

Kalman, Dan. "The Wrapping Function Kit." *Mathematics Teacher* 71 (September 1978): 516–17.

Laurent, Theresa. "'Drug' Reaction." Reader Reflections. *Mathematics Teacher* 99 (September 2005): 86.

Lesh, Richard, Tom Post, and Merlyn Behr. "Representations and Translations among Representations in Mathematics Learning and Problem Solving." In *Problems of Representation in the Teaching and Learning of Mathematics,* edited by Claude Janvier, pp. 33–40. Mahwah, N.J.: Erlbaum, 1987.

McGraw, Sue Ann, ed. *Integrated Mathematics: Choices and Challenges.* Reston, Va.: National Council of Teachers of Mathematics, 2003.

National Council of Teachers of Mathematics (NCTM). *Principles and Standards for School Mathematics.* Reston, Va.: NCTM, 2000.

National Research Council (NRC). *How People Learn: Brain, Mind, Experience, and School.* Expanded ed. Washington, D.C.: National Academy Press, 2000.

Polya, George. *How to Solve It: A New Aspect of Mathematical Method.* 3rd ed. Princeton, N.J.: Princeton University Press, 1973.

Brown, Richard. *Geometry and Algebra with Transformations.* Parts I and II. Los Angeles, Calif.: printed by the author with funding from the W. M. Keck Foundation, 1995.

Systemic Initiative for Montana Mathematics and Science (SIMMS). "What's Your Orbit?" In *SIMMS Integrated Mathematics,* Level 3, pp. 229–47. Dubuque, Iowa: Kendall/Hunt Publishing Co., 2003.

Suggested Reading

Hodgson, Ted R., and Maurice J. Burke. "Tennis Anyone?" *Mathematics Teacher* 98 (May 2005): 586–92.

Scher, Daniel. "Dynamic Visualization and Proof: A New Approach to a Classic Problem." *Mathematics Teacher* 96 (September 2003): 394–98.